BRITAIN'S LIVING HERITAGE

BRITAIN'S LIVING HERITAGE

PHILIP SAUVAIN

B. T. Batsford Ltd, London

Designed by Alan Hanıp. Typeset in Monophoto Sabon and printed in Great Britain by Butler & Tanner Ltd Frome and London for the publishers B. T. Batsford Ltd 4 Fitzhardinge Street London W1H 0AH

PAGE 1 *Sanctuary knocker at the entrance to Durham Cathedral.*

FRONTISPIECE *South doorway at Kilpeck Church.*

TITLE PAGE *Fifteenth-century misericorde carving at Lavenham in Suffolk showing a jester.*

THIS PAGE *The Houses of Parliament, built between 1840 and 1857.*

Contents

Prehistoric Britain

The Stone Age

The earliest period of human activity is known as the palaeolithic or Old Stone Age. If the palaeolithic people built structures in Britain they lacked permanence, for little is known of their settlements, other than that some remains have been discovered in caves and rock shelters, such as those at Cresswell Crags in Derbyshire and Kent's Cavern in Torbay.

About 10 000 years ago mesolithic (Middle Stone Age) people established a temporary settlement on a site at Star Carr near Scarborough in north Yorkshire. They laid down a brushwood platform across marshy ground and built rough shelters there. This was their temporary home while they fished in lakes using spears and bone hooks. They also hunted elk, red deer and wild pig. The skills of the mesolithic hunters were already quite considerable for they used hunting dogs, bows and arrows, flint knives, chisels, awls and axes.

Over 6500 years ago neolithic (New Stone Age) immigrant farmers from the Continent came to Britain. Evidence of the neolithic settlement has been found in many areas; in the discovery of pottery, flint tools and other artefacts, and in the structures the neolithic people erected, such as the chambered tomb of Trevethy Quoit in Cornwall.

One group of neolithic farmers lived in the vicinity of Avebury in Wiltshire in about 3000 BC, and erected a causewayed camp at Windmill Hill.

The earthworks, which they built to encircle the hill, may have delineated an area for use as a ceremonial meeting place, as a ritual burial site or possibly as a compound for a yearly round-up of their wide-horned cattle, sheep and pigs (identified from bones which had been deliberately buried on the site).

These neolithic people were the first farmers in Britain and they brought many skills with them besides a knowledge of farming. They were still in the Stone Age, however, since their tools were fashioned from stone, wood and bone. The sophistication of their culture can be seen from their flint mines and from their burial places.

At Grime's Graves in Norfolk they sank mine shafts about 20 to 30 feet deep and then used pick axes, made from the antlers of red deer, to excavate the flints which were embedded in the chalk. They may have used ladders made from wooden poles and strips of leather to climb down the shafts.

Prehistoric Burial Places

Much of what we know about the everyday life of people in prehistoric Britain comes from a study of funeral items, such as the ornaments, pottery and tools which have been discovered in the long barrows in which the neolithic people buried their dead. These were long mounds of earth, usually covering either a wooden or a stone burial chamber, which contained the remains of several individuals.

At West Kennet, near Avebury in Wiltshire, a particularly fine example of a neolithic long barrow held the remains of at least 46 people. This West Kennet long barrow, which is about 300 feet long and about 80 feet wide, was first built about 4500 years ago but the burials themselves took place over a long period of time. There were five stone burial chambers, linked by a central passageway, and the entrance to the tomb was eventually sealed by three large boulders. By any standards, the neolithic farmers who built West Kennet used considerable technical skill in its construction.

In the succeeding period of the Bronze Age round barrows were used, usually to hold the remains of a single individual – presumed to be a chieftain or other person of equivalent rank.

ABOVE LEFT *Trevethy Quoit – a neolithic burial chamber near Liskeard in Cornwall.*

LEFT *Deep hollow showing the position of a filled-in neolithic flint mine shaft at Grime's Graves near Thetford in Norfolk. The flint miners probably filled it with the earth they dug out of a new shaft close by.*

BELOW *Narrow galleries at the base of a mine shaft at Grime's Graves.*

Burial chamber (sometimes called a cromlech *or* dolmen) *near Criccieth in north Wales. Remains of individuals were placed in the chamber which was sealed by the capstone on top. It is possible the chamber was originally covered by a heap of stones and earth.*

Entrance to the stone burial chamber of the neolithic long barrow at West Kennet in Wiltshire.

Bronze Age round barrow near Stonehenge in Wiltshire.

Stone Circles and Henges

Stonehenge is the most visited and most celebrated prehistoric monument in Britain; yet it is only one among the many stone circles and wooden henge monuments, dating back to neolithic and Bronze Age times, which can be seen in Britain in places as far apart as Cornwall (the Merry Maidens stone circle) and Orkney (the Ring of Brodgar). Of these the most impressive is probably the huge stone circle and complex of earthworks at Avebury in Wiltshire, said to be the largest prehistoric monument in Europe, and estimated to have taken at least 1 500 000 man hours to build.

Stonehenge is the most sophisticated stone circle, however, since the scale and nature of the building there warrant the description of 'prehistoric cathedral' which has sometimes been applied to it. The concept of Stonehenge as a religious building is not necessarily refuted by modern theories which have demonstrated the mathematical and astronomical significance of the layout of the stones at Stonehenge and of other stone circles in Britain. Stonehenge could well have been both – a great temple and a place from which to observe the apparent movement of the sun, moon and planets.

At least three main building periods have been identified at Stonehenge, indicating a total building history of at least 1000 years. When completed about 3200 years ago it consisted of a central horseshoe of five huge trilithons composed of massive sarsen (sandstone) boulders. They can be seen in their rough form at Avebury but at Stonehenge they were carefully shaped by stone masons. Stone hammers and other tools were used to carve a protruding knob or tenon on the top of each upright stone so that it would fit into a mortise hole on the underside of the lintel stone which lay across each pair of uprights.

Inside this horseshoe of trilithons (meaning 'three stones') the Bronze Age people erected another horseshoe of smaller boulders, the bluestones from the Prescelly Mountains of south Wales. These two horseshoes were surrounded by an inner circle of bluestones and an outer circle of 30 upright sarsen stones with a continuous ring of curved lintel stones on top.

Set apart from the circle and standing on its own is the Heel Stone with its position precisely at the point where the sun appears to rise on Midsummer Day when viewed from the centre of the horseshoe. Computer studies have recently raised many other interesting possibilities and thrown new light on the nature of the civilization which was capable of erecting these stones and placing them so carefully in position.

Stone circle at Castlerigg near Keswick in Cumbria.

Stone circle at Avebury in Wiltshire. The steep bank in the background is also part of this huge prehistoric monument.

The outer circle of tall sarsen stones at Stonehenge. The smaller stones on the left are part of the inner circle of bluestones.

The Bronze Age

The first Bronze Age settlers came to Britain in about 2500 BC, bringing with them a new culture based on metal working in copper and later in bronze. Much later still, these Bronze Age farmers used a primitive plough, called an ard, which was pulled by oxen to cultivate small rectangular fields. These can be seen from the ground as minor undulations in the land, sometimes with marked terraces or ridges, called lynchets, dividing one field from another. On an Ordnance Survey map they are marked as Celtic Fields.

Remains of Bronze Age farming villages have been discovered at Itford Hill and Plumpton Plain in Sussex where post holes have enabled archaeologists to deduce the sort of huts and villages the farmers lived in. At Grimspound on Dartmoor, a large walled enclosure of about four acres contains the remains of some 20 to 30 round beehive huts, erected by Bronze Age farmers about 3000 years ago at a time when the climate of Dartmoor permitted cattle rearing.

The Iron Age

The Iron Age is broadly the period which began in the eighth and seventh centuries BC when different groups of people in Britain began to use iron tools and implements and at the same time developed new types of defensive settlements, known as hillforts.

Iron had two principal uses, for war (swords, axes, chariot wheels) and for tools (ploughshares, knives, cauldrons). The Iron Age peoples still continued to use bronze for many tools, ornaments and even for shields and helmets. They were warriors as well as farmers and erected many hillforts

Trilithons at Stonehenge. Notice the tall upright stone with the protruding knob or tenon.

BELOW *The Heel Stone at Stonehenge seen through the two uprights of a trilithon.*

as defensive settlements, such as those at Maiden Castle and Badbury Rings in Dorset.

The huge ramparts at Maiden Castle were originally topped by a spiked wooden fence or palisade. Three of these great earth circles surround the hill which is about 1000 yards long. Within the hillfort there were round wooden huts, storage pits for grain and hoards of stones for use in slings (their principal weapon).

The Iron Age peoples may also have been responsible for cutting some of the hill figures which have been carved in chalk. The Uffington White Horse in Oxfordshire is believed to be the earliest of these extraordinary features but there is some doubt whether the Long Man of Wilmington in Sussex dates from Iron Age or Saxon times.

An Iron Age Farm

The Butser Ancient Farm Project in the Queen Elizabeth Country Park near Petersfield in Hampshire is a fascinating full-scale working model of an Iron Age farm. It has been designed to throw light, through practical working experience, on what it was like to live in Britain in about 300 BC.

It consists of a village compound surrounded by a bank and ditch approximately six feet wide and five feet deep. A palisade tops the ramparts. In the Iron Age a fence like this was probably intended to keep out wild animals rather than hostile tribes. This compound has been based on earthworks at East Castle in Wiltshire. The large hut which dominates the site is also based on archaeological evidence – Iron Age post holes discovered at a site in Pimperne in Dorset. The post holes are the holes in the ground where the wooden supporting posts for a hut roof were originally erected. The timber has long since decayed but archaeologists can identify the position of these holes from stains and

other evidence, even after a period of 2000 years or more.

The Pimperne hut at Butser was constructed from oak posts interwoven with hazel laths and covered with an earth mixture of clay, hair and

TOP *Lynchets in Wensleydale in north Yorkshire. These banks or terraces were created when the fields were ploughed either in Bronze Age or Iron Age times or possibly even in early mediaeval times.*

ABOVE *Paved entrance to the Bronze Age village at Grimspound on Dartmoor.*

straw (called daub). The roof is supported by a ring of posts and thatched with straw.

On the farm the research team have conducted many other experiments such as smelting iron ore, keeping grain in storage pits in the ground, growing Iron Age crops such as emmer (a type of wheat) and rearing livestock like the Soay sheep from St Kilda whose bones most closely resemble those of prehistoric sheep found in archaeological excavations.

Inside the Pimperne hut there is a central oven made of clay and shaped like a beehive. Smoke from the oven makes its own way through the thatched roof. One interesting result of this experiment is that the team has found that the smoke not only escapes, it has a beneficial effect too, in that it clears insects from the straw and can be used to cure meat and animal skins.

The floor area of the hut is so vast that as many as 200 people can lie down on the floor. Huts like these were probably used in the Iron Age as communal halls or as the headquarters of a tribal chief.

Prehistoric Routeways

Geological or archaeological evidence which enables experts to identify flints from mines such as Grime's Graves, found many miles away from their source of origin, shows something of the extent to which prehistoric people travelled in order to obtain first-class flints for their tools and weapons.

Some of the routeways used by these prehistoric pedlars have been identified among the chalklands of southern England. The most famous of these prehistoric trackways is probably the Berkshire Ridgeway route which linked Wessex with East Anglia.

Peddars Way in Norfolk was certainly a Roman road which linked the Icknield Way to the fort at Brancaster. It may well have been built along the line of a much earlier prehistoric trackway, since a number of barrows follow the same general alignment of the route.

Hut circle at Grimspound. In Bronze Age times the granite walls would have been much higher than this, probably covered over with a roof of thatch or turf resting on a timber framework.

Reconstruction of an Iceni Iron Age village at Cockley Cley near Swaffham in Norfolk, showing the gateway.

BELOW *The Iron Age hill fort at Maiden Castle in Dorset.*

The Long Man of Wilmington.

Part of the ditch and earth bank which surrounds the Iron Age village reconstruction at Butser.

BELOW *The Pimperne house at Butser.*

Thatched haystacks within the compound of the village. They stand on a timber platform to enable air to circulate underneath.

Bowl furnace in the smelting area of the village compound. Charcoal was used to heat the iron ore which was later hammered into shape.

BELOW *Inside the Pimperne house.*

Stretch of Peddars Way near Snettisham in Norfolk.

Prehistoric clapper bridge at Postbridge in Devon. It is thought to date back to Bronze Age times.

Roman Britain

Boudicca (or Boadicea) was one of the first people to be born in Britain whose name is known as a matter of historical record. Her celebrated rebellion as leader of the Iceni in East Anglia in AD 60 is therefore appropriately (if inaccurately) commemorated in this splendid Edwardian statue in Westminster, close to the Houses of Parliament. Boudicca's rebellion was one of the few significant stands made by the Iron Age tribes against the Roman invaders.

Four legions led by Aulus Plautius landed at Richborough in Kent in AD 43. This was later the site of the most important of the Roman coastal forts of the Saxon shore. The Second Augustan Legion under Vespasian (later Emperor of Rome) drove south-westwards and inflicted a major defeat on the Iron Age people who tried to defend Maiden Castle. The heavy fortifications of the hillfort were more than adequate to meet the onslaught of similarly armed tribesmen but not to withstand the sophisticated might of the Roman army. Ballistae (a type of mechanical catapult) were used by the Romans to shower metal bolts into the fort before an infantry attack.

Eventually legionary fortresses were founded at York, Chester and Caerleon. A line linking these forts and extended to Exeter in the south roughly delimits the Roman Military Zone which lay to the north and west while the Civil Zone lay to the south and east. Broadly speaking the Military Zone is where one can expect to find the vast majority of Roman forts (with the notable exception of the coastal forts of south-eastern England) and the Civil Zone where one can see most of the villas, farms and towns. Unifying the whole are the Roman roads which define the extent of the Roman occupation of Britain.

Statue of Boudicca at the end of Westminster Bridge, London.

Hadrian's Wall

The most important Roman remains in Britain are to be seen along Hadrian's Wall which was built after AD 122, the year in which the Emperor Hadrian visited Britain. This impressive line of fortifications practically divides England from Scotland, stretching as it does from Bowness on the Solway in the west to Wallsend on the Tyne in the east. Hadrian ordered it to be built to keep out the barbarians.

The Wall is 73 miles long and varies in width and structure along its course. In places it is about ten feet wide and about 15 feet in height. Like most Roman buildings it was built to a strict plan with minor forts, called milecastles, situated every Roman mile (1620 yards) along the length of the wall. These were garrisoned by small detachments of about 30 soldiers. In between the milecastles, at intervals of about 540 yards, there were turrets or small towers which acted as lookout posts. If the enemy was sighted the soldiers on duty there lit fires to give warning to the other soldiers manning the wall.

At regular intervals there were major forts such as Housesteads, Chesters and Carrawburgh where battalions of up to 1000 men were posted. Sixteen of these forts were built along the line of the wall.

Roman Forts

From the air a Roman fort has the same shape as a squarish playing card with curved corners. Each fort usually has a grid of streets separating the main buildings, with two main roads bisecting the camp at right angles to each other. At the heart of the fort stood the headquarters building which was the nerve centre for the garrison stationed there. Close by stood the commandant's villa and other important central buildings such as the granaries and hospital.

Beyond the administrative centre there were barracks where the soldiers lived and stables for the horses. There were also storehouses, workshops, washrooms and latrines, while outside the main gates of the fort was the bath house and often civilian houses and shops run by the local inhabitants.

Surrounding the fort was a wall and a ditch. Most of these fortifications have collapsed or been used as a quarry of ready hewn stone in the intervening span of nearly 2000 years. Excellent remains of these walls can still be seen, however, at the coastal forts which were built in the third century when the coast was being repeatedly attacked by Saxon pirates.

The Romans had high sanitary standards. At the infantry fort of Housesteads on Hadrian's Wall, the soldiers had the benefit of a communal latrine. Channels of running water were used to rinse the sponges which the soldiers used instead of toilet paper. Basins were provided so they could wash their hands afterwards and running water also flushed the sewers.

Roman Villas

Many of the villas which have been excavated so far were owned by the Romano-British, the tribesmen who adopted the Roman way of life and who, in World War II terminology, might be regarded today as collaborators. Indeed the most magnificent of all the Roman residences so far discovered in Britain is believed to have been built for King Cogidubnus, tribal leader of the Atrebates. His magnificent palace at Fishbourne near Chichester was only discovered by accident in 1960.

The palace was begun in the first century and when it was complete featured walls inlaid with marble, exquisite mosaic floors, painted walls, elaborate friezes, verandahs, extensive hot and cold baths, a magnificent entrance hall with six columns and a huge audience chamber.

It has been preserved by erecting a large modern building which exactly covers the north wing of the palace. The box hedge seen in the photograph was planted in the same trenches which the Romans used, so that in effect Fishbourne today enables the visitor to see what a Roman garden

Hadrian's Wall from the Roman fort at Housesteads.

BELOW *Brunton Turret on Hadrian's Wall a few miles north of Hexham in Northumberland.*

looked like, when it was first planted 2000 years ago.

Several other Roman villas have been excavated, particularly in southern Britain, such as Lullingstone in Kent, Bignor in Sussex, Rockbourne in Hampshire and Chedworth in Gloucestershire. Like the forts, they tend to follow the same basic pattern. Most have an easily identified principal dining room with an elaborate mosaic floor. Other reception rooms are also floored with mosaic designs. The bedrooms and other living quarters are not so easily recognized but there is no mistaking the bath-house suite with its hot and cold baths.

One of the most distinctive features in a villa is the hypocaust central heating system which the

Romans used some 2000 years ahead of their time. This was an underfloor system with warm air circulating beneath the rooms from a furnace room nearby. Today the hypocaust system can be identified by the grid of stone pillars which formerly supported the floor, as in the room in the north wing of the Roman villa at Chedworth seen in the photograph on page 23.

Roman Towns

Roman towns were invariably built with a central administrative block, called the forum, at the heart of the town. This usually consisted of a market place with a basilica or meeting house at one end of the square and an arcade of shops on at least one of the other three sides. This was where the town's business affairs were conducted and where the Romans administered justice. Main roads usually crossed the town at right angles to one another and passed through gatehouses set between the massive walls which surrounded the town. An inn was often built near one of these gatehouses for the benefit of travellers. Other amenities in the town sometimes included a bath house, theatre or even a public lavatory.

Just outside the town the Romans sometimes built an amphitheatre. The amphitheatre they built at Dorchester is known today as Maumbury Rings. In Roman times it was probably used for parades and exhibitions and may even have been used by gladiators and wild beasts. A room close to the entrance to the arena could have been a cage for animals.

An unusual feature can be seen at Dover where a lighthouse (or *pharos*) helped to guide ships into the harbour. The lighthouse keepers probably lit

flares or fires at night which could have been seen from the coast of Gaul some 21 miles away.

Pride of place among the amenities of any Roman town was taken by the baths. This was a kind of sauna bath where hot rooms, hot baths, cold rooms and cold baths provided a range of different temperatures. Facilities were available for refreshments, physical exercise and massage. In particular oil was applied to the body and scraped off with the aid of a special tool called a *strigil*, as a way of cleansing the body.

The Great Bath at Bath was about 70 feet long, 30 feet wide, six feet deep, floored with lead sheeting and fed from a warm spring which kept the water at a constant temperature of 49°C (120°F). In Roman times the Great Bath was not open to the sky but covered instead by a huge semi-circular roof called a barrel vault.

In view of the Roman preoccupation with bathing it is hardly surprising to find a bath house close to Hadrian's Wall, for use by the soldiers stationed at the cavalry fort at Chesters.

Roman Roads

The Roman road system in Britain must have been the envy of any resident of ancient Rome. In Rome, the capital city of a great empire, the traffic problem became so acute that Julius Caesar had to ban wheeled traffic by day, with the inevitable result that people then complained about the traffic roar at night!

In Britain, by contrast, there were about 6000 miles of excellent road, well surfaced and generally built as straight as possible. Surveyors used an instrument called a *groma* in order to align the roads and the engineers dug ditches on

either side of the raised roadway, to ensure it was well drained. This substantial achievement was not to be equalled again until the construction of the better turnpike roads at the end of the eighteenth century.

One of the most impressive of the remains of these Roman roads can be seen at Wheeldale Moor, near Scarborough in north Yorkshire. When this road was constructed in Roman times, the slabs to be seen in the photograph on page 26 were only the foundation stones resting on a raised bank of earth, called the *agger*. When in use it would have been surfaced with fine gravel to produce a smooth finish suitable for use by carts and chariots.

LEFT *Water tank in the supply depot at Corbridge to the south of Hadrian's Wall.*

BELOW LEFT *West granary at the Corbridge supply depot showing the spaces below the flagstone floor which allowed air to circulate to keep the corn dry.*

WEST
GRANARY
SITE X

ABOVE *Flint and stone wall bordering the west wing of the Roman palace at Fishbourne near Chichester.*

Bath house for soldiers stationed at the cavalry fort of Chesters. The changing room in the foreground still retains the row of lockers (on the right) for their clothes.

RIGHT *Mosaic floor dating from the second century at Fishbourne Roman palace.*

ABOVE *Mosaic in the large dining room of the Roman villa at Chedworth. Each of the four corners of the mosaic depicts a season of the year. This one shows a girl representing spring, with a basket of flowers in her left hand and a bird on her right hand.*

RIGHT *Hypocaust in a room in the Roman villa at Chedworth in Gloucestershire.*

The Roman lighthouse or pharos *at Dover.*

LEFT *Part of the town wall which surrounded Roman London. The upper part of this wall is mediaeval but the lower part, identified by the four courses of red tiles seen on the left, is Roman and in excellent condition.*

BELOW *The amphitheatre of Maumbury Rings in Dorchester.*

The Great Bath at Bath.

Lead water pipe set in the limestone paving stones on the north side of the Great Bath at Bath.

Hot bath at the military bath house at the cavalry fort of Chesters on Hadrian's Wall.

Part of the 1¼-mile stretch of Roman road at Wheeldale Moor near Scarborough.

LEFT Roman milestone at Vindolanda on the Stanegate south of Hadrian's Wall.

Anglo-Saxon Britain

During the last 130 years of Roman rule in Britain, the coasts of south-eastern England were repeatedly attacked by Saxon sea-raiders from Denmark and northern Germany. In 367 and 369 the attacks became more serious. The Roman army eventually drove off the invaders but increasing barbarian attacks on other parts of the Roman empire impelled the Romans to withdraw their troops finally from Britain in about 407. British emissaries later went to Rome to urge the Romans to come to their aid, with a plea which talked of 'the groans of the Britons', but it fell on deaf ears.

From about 450 the first permanent Saxon settlements began to be established in East Anglia and Kent. The brothers Hengest and Horsa are traditionally supposed to have led the way when they landed at Ebbsfleet in 449 (see also page 33).

Despite the fact that the Saxons (and Angles and Jutes) lived in Britain for more than 600 years there is relatively little evidence on the ground today to show what it was like to live in Saxon times. This is partly because the Saxons, unlike the Romans, built primarily with wood rather than stone and therefore their buildings haven't survived. Their boats and homes were made of timber; indeed their homes have been described as being little more than upturned boats.

It was Christianity which was responsible for the most ubiquitous evidence of our Saxon heritage. Although the Saxons undoubtedly used timber for many of their churches, they also used stone as well. Only one of these timber churches has survived, at Greensted in Essex, but a surprisingly large number of churches throughout Britain have Saxon work somewhere in the structure or are of Saxon origin. Churchyard crosses and Celtic crosses (reflecting the Celtic Christianity of Ireland, Wales and Scotland) can also be seen diffused quite widely over Britain.

It is a remarkable fact too that almost all the settlement place-names of England owe their origin either to the Saxons or to the Danes. Many Saxon settlements can be identified from the place-name endings *ing, ham* and *ton. Ing* is a shortened form of *ingas* meaning 'people', while *ham* and *ton* signify hamlet, village or town. So

The Anglo-Saxon village at West Stow near Bury St Edmunds in Suffolk.

Rare example of a Saxon sundial above the entrance to the Saxon church at Bishopstone in Sussex.

FAR RIGHT *Where Bida had a pasture for swine in Kent (Bida's denn).*

Where 'Herela's people' settled in Norfolk.

Beorn's ley (pasture).

the hamlet of Snot's people was *Snot ingas ham* (Nottingham) and Hastings was the home of Haesta's people. Other settlements had endings like *ley* and *denn* which described a clearing in the forest used for pasture as at Barnsley (Beorn's *ley*) and Benenden (Bionna's *den*).

A Saxon Village

Archaeological evidence of Saxon homes is so scanty that even today there is insufficient data to be absolutely sure why some of their houses were built over a sunken pit. Was the floor of the pit the floor of the house? Or was it boarded over, like a modern house, to allow air to circulate underneath? Questions like these are being tested out in the field at the Anglo-Saxon village of West Stow near Bury St Edmunds in Suffolk, where archaeologists have reconstructed some of the actual homes which were excavated on the site there between 1965 and 1972.

These excavations uncovered the remains of about 80 wooden buildings of a Saxon village which had been occupied from about 450 to 650. The photograph shows in the centre the traditional idea of a Saxon dwelling as a lean-to, or tent-like building, with a pitched thatch roof over a sunken pit below ground level. To the right can be seen the more recent conception of a walled hut built over a pit which has been floored with timber – the space underneath allowing air to circulate and so act as a primitive damp-proof device.

ABOVE RIGHT *West Stow Anglo-Saxon village near Bury St Edmunds in Suffolk. The building on the right is a reconstruction of the communal hall which was the central meeting place for the people living in the houses and huts clustered around it.*

BELOW RIGHT *Different types of hut at West Stow.*

29

Whitby Abbey in north Yorkshire, founded by St Hilda in 657. It was later sacked by the Vikings and destroyed. The ruins to be seen today date from the period when the abbey was rebuilt after the Norman Conquest.

BELOW *Pictish symbols and ornamental cross on a 10-foot high stone slab at Fowlis Wester near Crieff in Perthshire.*

The Coming of Christianity

Christianity had first reached Britain in Roman times but the pagan Saxons drove British Christians towards the west. It was from this source that the Celtic Church developed. In the south the traditional beginning of the Anglo-Saxon conversion dates from 597 when St Augustine landed with 40 monks at Ebbsfleet in Kent.

Differences between the two types of Christianity were resolved at the Synod of Whitby in 664. This established that Roman practices were to be followed rather than those of the Celtic Church. The effect of Christianity on Saxon Britain was immeasurable. Monasteries were founded, scholars and monks like Bede flourished and many churches were built.

Monks who travelled the length and breadth of Britain preaching Chirstianity often did so at the side of the road where a wayside cross marked out the area as being a place of worship. These crosses were also sited in churchyards to show that this was holy ground.

Saxon cross in the churchyard at Eyam in Derbyshire, believed to date back to the ninth century.

Greensted Church near Chelmsford in Essex.

BELOW *Saxon church of St Lawrence in Bradford-on-Avon in Wiltshire – one of the oldest churches in Britain dating back to the end of the seventh century.*

Saxon Churches

With the solitary exception of the church of St Andrew in Greensted, only those Saxon churches built of stone have survived to the present day. This makes it all the more remarkable that this diminutive little church should still retain logs in the walls of its nave, which scientific tests have shown to be over 1000 years old.

Other parts of Greensted Church have been heavily restored. Most Saxon churches have undergone similar alterations so that it is rarely possible to picture them exactly as they were in Saxon times.

The overall style of the Saxons was simple and direct. Their doors and windows were generally small with either a sharply slanting triangular or rounded arch. Belfry windows are often found in pairs. Many churches have distinctive towers such as the helm tower at Sompting in Sussex or those, like Earls Barton in Northamptonshire, which were decorated with narrow strips of stone called pilaster strip or lesene.

The Viking Invasions

When the Saxons were themselves threatened by Danish (or popularly Viking) invaders, at the end of the eighth century and in the ninth century, they eventually had to cede a large part of northern and eastern Britain, which came to be known as the Danelaw because it was subject to Danish not English law.

The Vikings who settled there often gave their hamlets and villages names with distinctive Danish endings such as *by, thorp* and *toft* as in Derby, Scunthorpe and Lowestoft.

The Vikings, like the Saxons, also tended to build with timber rather than with stone, so the full extent of their settlement has yet to be known. One of the most exciting archaeological finds of

recent years was made by accident, when evidence of the Viking capital of Jorvik was discovered in the centre of York.

The tenth-century town of Jorvik was built on top of what remained of the Roman city of Eburacum which had last echoed to the sound of Roman soldiers some 500 years earlier.

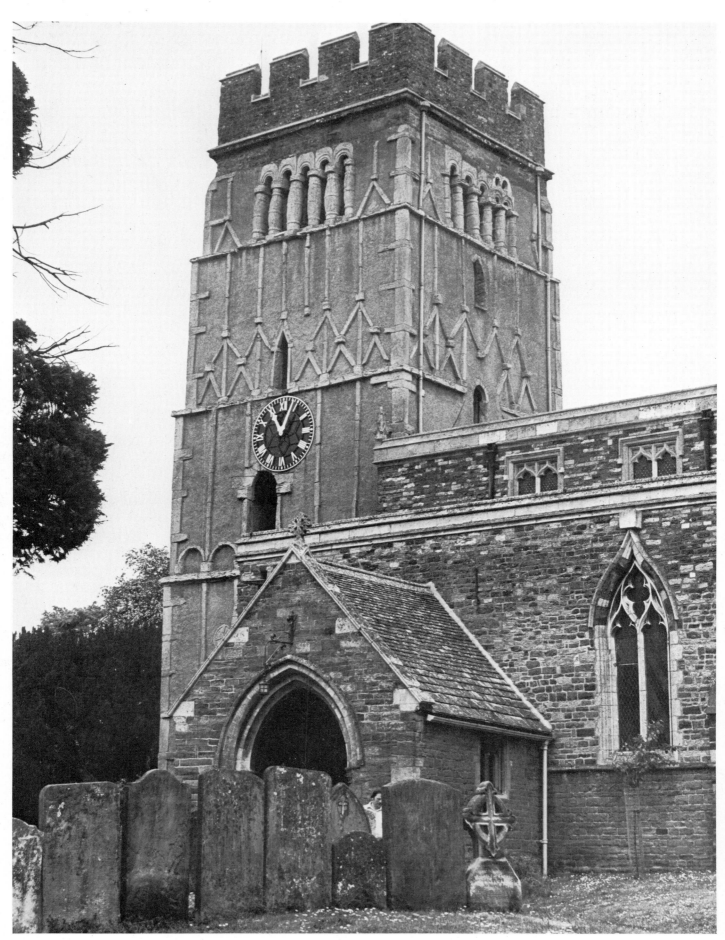

Saxon church at Earls Barton, Northamptonshire, particularly noted for its magnificent decorated tower believed to date back to the tenth century.

The excavations at the Coppergate site in York have uncovered substantial remains of Viking wooden buildings, usually with just one room measuring about 22 feet by ten feet. The walls were constructed of upright oak posts with horizontal wooden planks across, looking rather like the Saxon huts shown on page 29. It is assumed that the roofs of these buildings were either thatched or covered with wooden planks. Some buildings were made with walls of interwoven twigs covered with daub.

Rubbish tips and middens have also been found and these, together with the building sites, have yielded a rich source of finds including combs, cups, a board game, a complete shoe, padlock and keys.

LEFT *Stone at Swanage in Dorset commemorating a famous victory at sea, when according to* The Anglo-Saxon Chronicle *'there perished one hundred and twenty ships at Swanwich'.*

ABOVE *Village (by) in a clearing in the forest (ryos) near Bury St Edmunds, Suffolk.*

Full scale replica of a Viking longboat at Pegwell Bay in Kent. It was sailed from Denmark to Kent in 1949 to celebrate the 1500th anniversary of the landing of Hengest and Horsa in 449.

The Battle of Hastings

The battle of Hastings began on 14 October 1066 at about 9.00 a.m. It took place on a site about six miles to the north-west of Hastings, where Duke William of Normandy had assembled his army after landing at Pevensey on 28 September. King Harold had fought and won the battle of Stamford Bridge, against the Norwegian King Harald Hardrada, only three days earlier. The Saxon army had to march south in a hurry. On the morning of 14 October Harold's soldiers took up position on Senlac Hill and looked across the countryside shown in the photograph. In the distance the Norman army was drawn up on Telham Hill and when they advanced they came across the terrain seen in the foreground.

The course of the battle has been told many times, particularly in conjunction with the graphic battle scenes depicted on the Bayeux Tapestry, which led to the long-perpetuated idea that Harold was killed by a Norman arrow. The manner of his death is hardly of earth-shattering consequence so much as the fact of it; for this was the last time that the leader of a conquering army would land in England and seize power by force of arms.

RIGHT The face of a Norman! One of the bearded faces at the corners of the Norman font in the church at Altarnon in Cornwall.

ABOVE *The site of the battle of Hastings.*

Pegs staking out the position of Viking houses at the Coppergate site in York.

Mediaeval Britain

Tradition has it that before his victory at the battle of Hastings, Duke William vowed to build an abbey if he became king. True to his word he erected Battle Abbey on Senlac Hill, with the high altar marking the spot where King Harold had been killed.

This strong link between the Church and the mainstream of British history was emphasized repeatedly throughout the Middle Ages. Sometimes Crown and Church worked in unison; often they were in conflict. Defending the faith could prove tiresome. Henry II attempted to resolve the trouble he had encountered with a too-powerful Church by making his friend Thomas Becket the Archbishop of Canterbury. As is well known, Becket defended the Church against the Crown and the subsequent quarrel ended with the murder of Becket in 1170.

The spot where Becket fell can be seen in Canterbury Cathedral. The cathedral soon became a shrine for pilgrims throughout Europe and the martyrdom was also commemorated in mediaeval carvings such as the misericorde which can be seen in the church of Fornham St Martin in Suffolk.

William the Conqueror was crowned king on Christmas Day 1066 in Westminster Abbey, the great church founded by the penultimate king of the Saxons, Edward the Confessor. Since William's coronation the abbey has always been the traditional place for the coronation of English kings and queens.

The structure of Westminster Abbey today bears very little resemblance to the abbey which Edward and William knew. But no other building or site in Britain so perfectly embodies the living heritage of Britain. It is here (and to some extent in St Paul's also) that almost all the great men and women who have shaped British history lie buried or commemorated in stone.

Relatively few remains enshrine the long and futile efforts of the Crusaders to gain control of the Holy Land. Apart from the town of Baldock in Hertfordshire, which is believed to derive its name from Baghdad, and a number of inns named The Saracen's Head, there is little to show apart from Crusader churches like the twelfth-century Temple Church off Fleet Street. This is one of only four such churches in Britain and, like all the others founded by the Knights Templar, is circular in design, being modelled on the Church of the Holy Sepulchre in Jerusalem.

Campaigns overseas necessitated heavy taxes at

Gatehouse of Battle Abbey, Sussex.

TOP *Westminster Abbey.*

TOP RIGHT *The Temple Church.*

ABOVE *Fortified vicarage at Elsdon in Northumberland.*

ABOVE RIGHT *Memorial cross to the soldiers killed at the battle of Towton near York.*

home. It was this which helped to fuel the resolution of Cardinal Langton and the barons to secure King John's agreement to the terms of Magna Carta. A plaque, close to the high altar in the ruins of the great abbey of Bury St Edmunds, shows the place where this determination took on the character of a vow. A memorial at Runnymede in Surrey marks the spot where the charter was sealed.

There are many other indicators to highlight the turbulence of mediaeval Britain. The long border wars between England and Scotland forced the local inhabitants in both countries to take precautions, like the priests in Corbridge and Elsdon in Northumberland who fortified their homes.

Memorials to those who died in the great battles of the Middle Ages can also be seen, such as Neville's Cross in Durham, or the isolated cross in a field near Towton outside York, where 20 000 to 30 000 men died in a solitary day's fighting during the Wars of the Roses. This was in 1461 at a time when guns were already being used in warfare, like the fifteenth-century bombard (a cannon which fired stone balls) found in the moat at Bodiam Castle in Sussex.

Mediaeval Castles

William the Conqueror's first move, after defeating Harold at the battle of Hastings, was to capture Dover and strengthen the castle there. Later in the reign of Henry II (1154–1189) work was started on the magnificent stone castle which dominates the town today.

The first Norman castles were invariably wooden keeps surmounting a natural or manmade hill. A ditch was dug all the way around the site and earth piled up in the middle to form a *motte*. A wooden palisade enclosed a large courtyard or bailey around the keep. This is why these early castles are called motte and bailey castles. All the wooden structures have long since decayed or disappeared but many of the mottes on which they stood can still be seen. Particularly striking mottes are those on which stone castles were later built as replacements for the earlier wooden fortifications. Both Clifford's Tower in York and the hollow shell keep at Arundel Castle are built on mottes of this type. The shell of the keep often followed the line of the original wooden palisade.

The early keeps and towers were square-sided like those at Dover Castle but castle engineers soon discovered that curved walls and circular towers could resist the undermining techniques of the trained siege engineer more effectively than those which had corners. Consequently many of the castles built in the thirteenth century and later have round towers. Later castle builders concentrated on making the outer wall as strong as possible to make a curtain of defence.

Curtain wall castles of this type featured a number of strong towers often at the corners of the walls and these housed the living quarters, kitchens, storehouses and other essential buildings. In earlier castles these functions were concentrated in a strong central tower or keep.

A later development of the curtain wall castle was to provide an inner and an outer curtain wall. This concentric pattern reached perfection in the castles erected by Edward I in north Wales at the end of the thirteenth century.

Castles by this time had become very sophisticated and not only had a strong gatehouse but even outer gatehouses, called barbicans, through which an enemy had to pass to get to the main castle.

Visiting a castle today is often seen as a romantic trip into the past, since ruins often make a picturesque display in juxtaposition with the monotony of modern Britain. It is easy to forget that their fortifications were built in deadly earnest. The machicolations were not picturesque decorations but the means by which castle defenders could blind, maim or kill their enemies by pouring

TOP *Fifteenth-century cannon at Bodiam Castle in Sussex.*

ABOVE *Keep and curtain wall at Dover Castle in Kent.*

BELOW *Shell keep and motte at Arundel Castle in Sussex.*

RIGHT *Bodiam Castle in Sussex.*

ABOVE *Portcullis at Hever Castle in Kent. The spiked wooden gate ran in grooves in the wall on either side.*

RIGHT *Heavily fortified barbican at Lewes Castle in Sussex.*

boiling water, oil or lead through the murder holes below the battlements. They knew that if the castle was captured the besieging army would put them to death. Chivalry took rather peculiar forms in the Middle Ages.

It must always be remembered too that castles were homes, not only for the baron and his family but also for the soldiers and servants who helped it to function smoothly. For these castle retainers the most important room in the castle was the Great Hall where meals were eaten and where they sometimes slept on the floor.

Mediaeval Churches

Britain's mediaeval churches often present a riddle to the unwary visitor, since the fact that a guide-book refers to them as Norman or Perpendicular is not always borne out completely by an examination of the structure today – unlike the church at Lavenham shown on page 40.

Most churches have been restored and altered at different times since their time of origin. Some of the restorations are in the same style as the original, some are in the style prevalent at the time of the restoration and some are in an imagined style such as mock-Gothic.

The photograph showing the great Norman arch in the west end of Tewkesbury Abbey is a case in point. The huge window in the Perpendicular style which occupies the opening was inserted in 1686 after the wall had collapsed. It is not therefore in the style of the original Norman arch which surrounds it, nor is it a genuine window from the Perpendicular period (1350–1550).

Most churches and religious buildings mix different styles of building and architecture and it is often extremely difficult for anyone other than an expert to say whether a feature is genuine or not.

There is little doubt, however, that the most widespread and most easily accessible evidence of Britain's mediaeval heritage is to be seen in her countless churches, abbeys and cathedrals. They are not only interesting in their own right as buildings but also because they often reveal something of the everyday life of the people who lived in the Middle Ages. Carvings in wood and stone, stained glass, effigies, decorated fonts, brasses, memorials and wall paintings present a vivid and lively picture of everyday life in the fields, in the home and at work.

Some churches have a grimmer tale to tell. A part of the churchyard at Sandhurst in Kent is said to have been used as a plague pit to bury people who perished during the Black Death in 1348–9. The elaborate Sanctuary knocker on the door of Durham Cathedral, like those in other churches, enabled a fugitive from justice, who managed to evade his or her would-be captors, to gain temporary sanctuary inside the church.

Kilpeck Church in Herefordshire has been described by Nikolaus Pevsner as 'one of the most

perfect Norman village churches in England'. Round the south doorway arch are many magnificently detailed carvings in red sandstone featuring dragons, fish, birds and other creatures. The corbels below the roof are also decorated with representations of many different scenes, including the amusing pair of heads showing a rather doleful-looking dog and a wistful-looking rabbit.

TOP *Machicolations (murder holes) at Bodiam Castle in Sussex. Boiling water, red hot sand and other lethal substances could be poured through the holes on to enemies underneath.*

ABOVE *The Great Hall at Harlech Castle, Gwynedd.*

LEFT *Perpendicular window and Norman arch at Tewkesbury Abbey, Gloucestershire.*

Abbeys and Priories

The monasteries and priories played an important part in the economy of mediaeval Britain. Not only did they provide alms and help for the poor, in a sense supplying the sort of services the modern welfare state provides, but they also offered hospitality to travellers. Many monasteries had great farms and the Cistercian abbeys, in particular,

LEFT *Lincoln Cathedral – we owe the appearance of the west front to a succession of architects from the Norman period in about 1072 to that of the Perpendicular in the fifteenth century.*

ABOVE *Perpendicular church at Lavenham in Suffolk – almost all of it built between 1485 and 1525.*

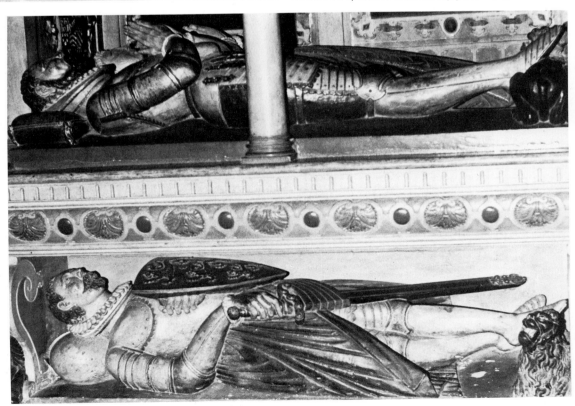

Effigies of fourteenth-century cross-legged knights in Exeter Cathedral.

FAR LEFT *Sixteenth-century brass monument at Stratton Church in Cornwall.*

ABOVE *Churchyard at Sandhurst, Kent.*

LEFT *Kilpeck Church, Herefordshire. Corbel with stone carvings of a dog and a rabbit.*

FAR LEFT *South doorway at Kilpeck Church – stone carving of a fox.*

BELOW *South doorway at Kilpeck Church – stone carving of fish.*

were noted for their great flocks of sheep in the later Middle Ages.

Most abbey buildings were built to the same general plan with the abbey church aligned from west to east and the cloister square (or garth) to the south. On the eastern side of the cloisters, immediately adjacent to the church, you can normally expect to find the chapter house where the monks or nuns met each day to attend to the business of their convent and to hear a reading of a chapter from the Rule of their religious order. In a Cistercian monastery the dormitory for the

monks was on this eastern side of the cloisters, often on the upper floor of a building next to the chapter house. Sometimes the dormitory was linked to the church by a flight of night stairs which meant that the monks didn't have to go outside in the cold night air when attending Matins in the early hours of the morning.

On the south side of the cloister garth stood the refectory or frater where the members of the convent ate their meals. Many refectories had serving hatches through to the adjacent kitchens. Outside the refectory there was usually a line of wash-basins (laver) together with cupboards, called aumbries, where the dry towels were kept. The sanitary arrangements in most mediaeval abbeys and priories were of a high order of excellence and far superior to those in use outside. The reredorter at Monk Bretton Priory near Barnsley provided the monks there with the facilities of a flush toilet. Water was ponded back by a penstock (temporary dam) and then released to flow down the sewer and drain the waste away.

Mediaeval Farming

Clues to the type of life lived on a mediaeval manor can sometimes be gleaned from the modern countryside. Many fields now in permanent pasture are ridged in a regular pattern. This is clearly seen from the air but only highlighted at ground level when the slanting rays of the early morning or early evening sun emphasize the alternating pattern of ridges and furrows in the fields, or when winter snow lies in the hollows producing a striped effect.

This ridge and furrow pattern was the result of

Interior of the church at Tintern Abbey, Gwent.

BELOW *The cloisters of Norwich Cathedral Priory.*

TOP *Serving hatch from the kitchens to the refectory at Monk Bretton Priory near Barnsley.*

ABOVE *Wall oven at Monk Bretton Priory. A wood fire was lit inside and when the ashes were white hot they were raked aside and bread and pasties pushed inside the oven on a long scoop.*

Reredorter at Monk Bretton Priory.

BELOW *The great thirteenth-century tithe barn at Great Coxwell in Oxfordshire.*

Ridge and furrow in a field at Milbourne near Newcastle-upon-Tyne.

Twelfth-century lead font at Brookland in Kent depicting the seasons. On the left cutting hay in June, making hay in July in the centre and cutting corn in August on the right.

mediaeval ploughing methods and dates back to the time of the open field system when each peasant held strips of land in each of the two or three great open fields of the manor. In return the peasant provided the lord of the manor with so many days work each week. In addition to this tax on his labour the mediaeval peasant also had to give a tenth part of his produce to the church (called a tithe). To this end huge barns were built to collect the tribute. Many splendid tithe barns can be seen today, such as those at Bradford-on-

Avon in Wiltshire or at Great Coxwell in Oxford-shire.

The farming methods and animals reared by mediaeval peasant farmers can sometimes be seen in church carvings. Some were etched on to the sides of the font or on the carved wooden ends of pews (bench ends) or on the underside of a tip-up seat (misericorde) which provided elderly clergy-men and monks with a small amount of practical support during long church services.

A Mediaeval Manor

Castles were the homes of great lords. Lesser lords and knights usually lived in fortified manor houses. Many were built of wood, with the result that they have long since decayed and been re-placed by later buildings. Some stone manor houses survive, however, such as the beautiful moated manor house of Ightham Mote near Sevenoaks in Kent.

This house is completely surrounded by a wide moat and the entrance, over a stone bridge, is through the massive oak doors of the fortified gatehouse to the cobbled courtyard beyond. The main room, like those in most castles and mediae-val farmhouses, is the great hall. At Ightham Mote this is nearly 40 feet in height, 30 feet in length and 20 feet in width. Other rooms include a chapel, a dungeon and a solar (or private living quarters).

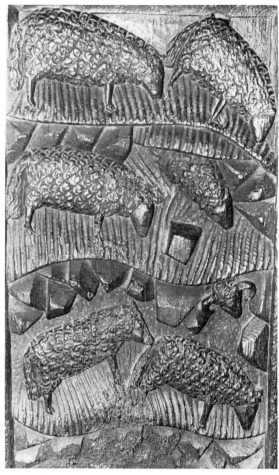

ABOVE *Early sixteenth-century carved bench end at Altarnon in Cornwall showing sheep grazing on a hillside.*

TOP RIGHT *Fifteenth-century misericorde carving at Fairford in Gloucestershire showing reapers with a sheaf of wheat.*

RIGHT *Fifteenth-century misericorde carving at Lavenham in Suffolk showing a man with a pig.*

Mediaeval Cottages

Most of the cottages built by mediaeval peasants have long since disappeared or been incorporated into later buildings. The building materials a peasant could afford, and the building techniques employed, were obviously fairly crude and insufficiently durable to withstand the ravages of five or six hundred years.

Fortunately a few of these buildings have been rescued and restored to something like their former state. Museums where Britain's living history can be enjoyed in the open include the Avoncroft Museum of Buildings in Bromsgrove and the Weald and Downland Museum at Singleton near Chichester.

The Weald and Downland Museum is situated amid the South Downs and here, in an imaginative setting, a number of mediaeval homes have been re-erected, after careful removal from their original sites somewhere in Kent or Sussex. Each house has been furnished so that it looks something like it did when it was occupied in the Middle Ages.

Mediaeval Towns

Although the mediaeval towns were largely composed of timber houses which have long since been pulled down, there are still many buildings from the fifteenth and early sixteenth centuries to enable us to imagine what it was like to live in a mediaeval town. The Little Hall, shown in the photograph (page 48), is in Lavenham in Suffolk, probably most perfectly preserved mediaeval and Tudor town in Britain. This was the home of a wealthy cloth merchant and was erected in the fourteenth century towards the end of the Middle Ages.

Houses of Norman age are much rarer and the two shown on pages 48 and 49 are almost unique for this reason. Both are traditionally supposed to have been owned by wealthy Jews in about 1180 but there is some reason to doubt this.

Bury St Edmunds was planned as a new town in the eleventh century. Abbot Baldwin designed the town on rectilinear lines and the streets to this day betray his grid plan. The great abbey dominated the town and a large open space was left to separate the town from the convent. This was

where the town's fairs were held; it was later transformed into the fine Georgian square known as Angel Hill.

Town Walls and Gates

Many mediaeval towns were open. That is to say they did not have town walls or gates and there were no restrictions on people leaving or entering these towns. Cities and towns which did have walls range in number and character from the busy industrial city of Newcastle-upon-Tyne to the historic cathedral cities of Canterbury, York, Norwich and Exeter.

The gates to a town were shut at night and often manned by soldiers. In 1282 new regulations came into force in the City of London. 'All the Gates of the City are to be open by day; and at each Gate there are to be two sergeants to open them and to keep a good watch upon persons coming in and going out.'

Many gatehouses incorporated a tollhouse where travellers passing through the gates had to pay a toll according to their type of vehicle and depending upon the goods they were bringing into

LEFT *Fifteenth-century stone gatehouse at Ightham Mote in Kent. The moat is between 20 and 30 feet in width.*

Courtyard at Ightham Mote showing the fourteenth-century Great Hall with its Decorated archway and Perpendicular window.

LEFT *Winkhurst – a late fourteenth-century farmhouse at Singleton. There is a communal hall at one end reaching to the roof. The smoke from the fire in the central hearth makes its way through a hole in the roof. There are three small glassless windows. At the other end there is a ground floor room and above it a solar or bedroom. The house originally came from Edenbridge in Kent.*

the town to sell. At Newark in Nottinghamshire these tolls were used to pay for paving the town's streets.

ABOVE *Hangleton Cottage – a reconstruction of a simple peasant's cottage at the Weald and Downland Open Air Museum at Singleton in Sussex. It has two ground floor rooms only.*

Bayleaf – a fifteenth-century Wealden farmhouse at Singleton. This was constructed with a timber frame, like Winkhurst, wattle and daub walls and glassless mullioned windows. The communal hall is in the centre of the house and reaches to the roof. To one side there is a ground floor parlour and to the other a kitchen and pantry. On the upper floor there are two bedchambers.

A *fifteenth-century wool merchant's house at Lavenham in Suffolk.*

Jew's House in Lincoln – a stone-built twelfth-century town house.

Moyses Hall – a flint and stone house built in the twelfth century in Bury St Edmunds in Suffolk.

Bootham Bar in York – one of the four mediaeval gateways to the city.

Section of London's mediaeval town wall near the Barbican.

The Southgait in St Andrews, Fifeshire. The mediaeval gateway to a Scottish city.

Mediaeval Ports

Most of the important towns of mediaeval Britain were ports trading with the continent. Towns which today are no longer in the front rank were of national importance then, such as King's Lynn at the mouth of the Great Ouse in Norfolk.

King's Lynn was a member of the Hanseatic League, or Hanse, an association of trading towns around the North Sea which included major European ports such as Hamburg, Lubeck, Danzig, Bergen, Bruges and London. Other merchants in Britain belonged to a rival organization known as the Merchant Adventurers and they too traded throughout Europe.

Merchants' homes can be seen in many mediaeval towns such as Hampton Court in King's Lynn, Strangers Hall in Norwich and Paycocke's House in Coggeshall in Essex. At King's Lynn there are mediaeval warehouses on the quayside and a splendid lookout tower which enabled the merchant to see across the fenland to the distant Wash to keep an eye open for his returning merchant ships.

The fourteenth-century Merchant Adventurers' Hall in York.

ABOVE *Woolpack with the monogram JG and merchant ship depicted in stone carvings outside Tiverton parish church in Devon. They were commissioned by a rich wool merchant called John Greenway in 1517.*

BELOW *Early sixteenth-century carved bench end at Bishops Lydeard in Somerset.*

Some idea of the nature of trade in mediaeval times can be seen in clues, such as the decorations on the parish church at Tiverton in Devon or the bench end in the church in Bishops Lydeard in Somerset.

The Guilds

The organization of each craft or trade was undertaken by a guild in the Middle Ages. The guild carefully controlled entrance to the craft and through an apprenticeship scheme ensured that all new recruits to the industry were properly trained. Each apprentice had to pass a test at the end of his apprenticeship at which he produced his 'master piece' for examination by the senior members of the guild.

These craft guilds have sometimes been likened to trade unions since they operated a rigid closed shop and laid down strict codes of behaviour for their members. However, since they were guilds of merchants, tradesmen and craftsmen they are more directly comparable with professional associations such as those of doctors or solicitors.

Some guilds were founded for charitable, religious or social purposes and members organized pageants and mystery plays, cared for their sick and aged members and devoted time, energy and money to religious projects such as the endowment of a chantry chapel or a church extension.

Many mediaeval guildhalls can still be found in the historic towns of Britain. Some, like the guildhall at Thaxted, were also used as market halls and some, like the guildhall in Norwich, became town halls.

ABOVE RIGHT *Fifteenth-century flint guildhall in Norwich.*

RIGHT *Fifteenth-century guildhall in Thaxted in Essex used by a guild of cutlers.*

BELOW *The early sixteenth-century half-timbered Guildhall of the Guild of Corpus Christi in Lavenham, Suffolk.*

Mediaeval Industry

Wool was at the heart of Britain's export trade in the Middle Ages, at first as bales of raw wool and later on as woollen cloth. The manufacture of the cloth was organized as a domestic industry in which almost all of the manufacturing processes were carried out in small cottages.

Each week the cloth merchant provided the craftsman with a bale of wool which he and his relatives first spun into woollen yarn and later wove into cloth. At the end of the week the clothier collected the piece of cloth and left a fresh bale of wool. The cloth was then taken to a fulling mill to be cleaned and was later finished by a cloth finisher such as the one shown in the carving on page 66.

Evidence of the mediaeval woollen industry can be seen in many different places such as the stone carving of a bale of wool at Tiverton (page 50) or the packhorse carrying bales of wool at the Wool-pack Inn (page 59). Spinners are sometimes shown in wood carvings and weavers' cottages are to be found in many areas once famous for their woollen cloth. The woollen merchants of Lavenham in Suffolk had their own trade mark, still to be seen today embossed in plasterwork on one or two buildings.

Although there were no factories in the modern sense of the word there were many windmills and watermills. Most of the watermills were used to grind corn into flour but some were used for other industrial purposes as well, such as turning grind-stones to sharpen knives or to drive the hammers in a fulling mill. Fulling was the process in which woollen cloth was washed and beaten to thicken it and make it more compact.

We know what mediaeval windmills looked like from church carvings and from illustrations in mediaeval manuscripts. The working windmill at

RIGHT *Fleur-de-lys embossed in plaster on the wall of the Swan Hotel in Lavenham. This was the Lavenham wool merchants' trade mark.*

BELOW *Row of fifteenth-century weavers' cottages in Lavenham, Suffolk.*

Great Chishill in the photograph (page 54) was built much later, in the early years of the nineteenth century, but is typical of many of the windmills in use in the past.

ABOVE *Fifteenth-century misericorde carving at Fairford church in Gloucestershire showing a woman spinning wool while her dog samples the stew in the cauldron!*

RIGHT *Early sixteenth-century bench end at Bishops Lydeard in Somerset showing a postmill.*

BELOW *Windmill depicted on a roof boss in the cloisters of Norwich Cathedral Priory.*

Early nineteenth-century postmill with fantail at Great Chishill in Cambridgeshire.

ABOVE RIGHT *Maypole on the village green at Aldborough in North York-shire.*

BELOW RIGHT *Morris dan-cers at Bourton-on-the-Water in Gloucestershire.*

Mediaeval Entertainments

The village green at Aldborough in north York-shire is dominated by the maypole, one of the few village green maypoles still left in Britain. At one time most villages would have had such a pole. At the other side of the green at Aldborough stands the Court House with the stocks in front. The public infliction of punishment on offenders was undoubtedly an entertainment in the Middle Ages, as it was right up to the middle of the nineteenth century. Cruel entertainments took many other forms such as the baiting of bears and bulls. Street signs still recall these days, such as the Bull Ring in Wakefield or The Bear Gardens in London.

Some mediaeval entertainments had a more ser-ious purpose. Every villager was required to prac-tise his skill at the butts – the archery grounds. This too is often commemorated in a street name. In St Andrews the butts is now a recreational area centred round a bandstand and in Appleby in Cumbria a notice proclaims 'Butts Car Park'. At Offham in Kent the local youths practised the art of tilting at the quintain. The contestants aimed at the flat studded target area. If they missed it they were usually struck by it anyway and if they scored a direct hit they had to be nimble to avoid the weight on the other end of the pivot swinging round and hitting them in the back. Tournament

grounds where knights participated can still be seen in some places such as in the grounds of Arundel Castle in Sussex.

Entertainments by travelling performers were also part of the everyday life of people living in the Middle Ages. In York and other towns actors, dressed up to represent biblical characters, per-formed Mystery Plays although these were often very funny and full of slapstick comedy. The ac-tors performed on a travelling stage called a pa-geant. This was a wagon with a platform about six feet off the ground which allowed the space underneath to be used for stage effects and as a dressing room. It was on wheels so that it could be taken from one street to another. In York the plays were staged in twelve different parts of the city.

Misericorde carvings, such as those shown on the title page and on page 56 from Lavenham Church, often feature jesters and musicians. The violinist at Altarnon Church in Cornwall was carved in the early sixteenth century on the end of a pew. Another bench end in the same church shows a bagpiper.

The quintain at Offham in Kent.

ABOVE *Early sixteenth-century bench end at Altarnon in Cornwall depicting a violinist.*

Fifteenth-century misericorde carving at Lavenham in Suffolk showing a pair of musicians – although the one on the left is said to be using a pair of tongs instead of a bow, and bellows instead of a violin!

Punishments of The Past

The most widespread form of punishment, still to be seen in many towns and villages, was the stocks. This was sometimes used, like a prison, to detain someone for several hours before taking further action. Many different types of stocks can be seen throughout Britain. Some were designed so that one of the uprights could be used as a whipping post, as at Docking in Norfolk. Pillories, where the victim stood with his or her head in a central hole and the two arms in adjacent holes, are relatively rare, however. Probably the best known example is at Coleshill in Warwickshire but others can be seen in Looe in Cornwall and Saffron Walden in Essex.

The ducking stool at Canterbury may seem an amusing device but hardly so for the unfortunate women, many of them in their old age, who were unceremoniously strapped into these chairs and plunged screaming into the cold polluted water of a pond or river.

The harshness of mediaeval justice can also be seen in the relics recalling the gibbet and the gallows. Halifax has a Gibbet Street and one of the main streets in the centre of Newcastle-upon-Tyne is called the Gallowgate. Some 30 miles to the north-west of Newcastle the passer-by can see, as he was intended to see in the past, the grim gibbet at Steng Cross overlooking the bleak moors of Northumberland. Another gibbet, much shorter in length, stands at the side of the road in Caxton in Cambridgeshire.

At Hexham in Northumberland there is a rela-

Village stocks at Stow-on-the-Wold, Gloucestershire.

Stocks and whipping post at Docking in Norfolk.

FAR LEFT *The gibbet at Steng Cross near Elsdon in Northumberland. William Winter was hanged here in 1791.*

LEFT *The gibbet at Caxton, Cambridgeshire.*

tively rare example of a mediaeval prison which was built between 1330 and 1332. Most castles, of course, had their own dungeons. At Carlisle Castle, one of the most interesting features to be seen is the wall covered with carvings scratched by prisoners in the fourteenth and fifteenth centuries depicting animals and biblical scenes.

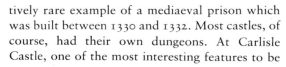

ABOVE LEFT *Ducking stool at Canterbury in Kent.*

BELOW LEFT *The fourteenth-century prison in Hexham, Northumberland.*

Mediaeval Travellers

Travellers usually went on foot or on horseback. The very rich sometimes travelled in a horse litter – rather like a sedan chair but with the shafts carried by horses rather than chairmen. Wealthy nobles, great abbots and bishops often travelled with a great entourage. Thomas Becket went on a journey in 1158 accompanied by eight carriages, 12 packhorses and about 200 servants.

Travel was slow and tedious because the roads were in an appalling condition and deep ruts and potholes made it almost impossible for wheeled traffic to travel far. Goods were usually carried by packhorses with the load slung on either side of the horse or pony. Often the only way of carrying goods over any distance was by boat.

There are few relics of mediaeval travel today apart from inn signs and a handful of inns which can trace their origins back to the fifteenth century or earlier. The most impressive evidence lies in the mediaeval bridges whose substance suggests that perhaps the routeways were not quite as bad as they are generally described. One or two bridges have other buildings standing on them such as the chapels on bridges in Wakefield and Rotherham, the tollhouse at Bradford on Avon and the gatehouse on the Monnow bridge at Monmouth.

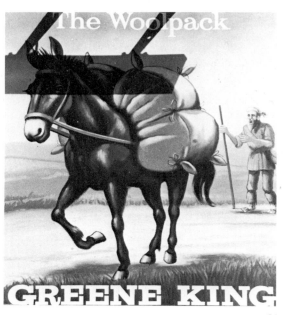

Inn sign at Fornham St Martin in Suffolk.

TOP *Rare example of a fortified mediaeval bridge – the Monnow Bridge in Monmouth, Gwent.*

ABOVE *Mediaeval bridge at Sturminster Newton, Dorset.*

Tudor Britain

When Henry VII came to the throne in 1485 he became king at a time when Europe was changing from a mediaeval to a modern society. The Italian Renaissance, the Protestant Reformation and the systematic exploration and discovery of the world by the Cabots, Columbus, Vasco da Gama, Magellan, Drake and many others were some of the changes which were to have a great impact on Britain.

Henry VII won the Crown after defeating and killing Richard III at the battle of Bosworth Field.

Statue of Sir Francis Drake on Plymouth Hoe.

His victory effectively brought to an end the Wars of the Roses which had decimated the aristocratic houses of England. This was the reason why Henry and the succeeding Tudor monarchs were able to establish strong and effective central government in England. Part of Henry VIII's concern for a male heir sprang from the thought that the accession of a queen might be disputed. In fact it was the reign of his rejected daughter, Elizabeth, which was to establish England in the forefront of European nations. Sir Francis Drake was one of a number of outstanding people (Frobisher, Hawkins, Grenville, Raleigh) who made the reign of Elizabeth a golden age at sea, while in the theatre Shakespeare, Jonson and Marlowe were also leaving their own mark.

The living heritage of Tudor Britain can be experienced in most parts of the country – from the carved Tudor bench ends at Altarnon in Cornwall (depicting everyday life in the period 1510 to 1530) to the moated manor house of Hever Castle in Kent where Henry VIII courted Anne Boleyn. Anne was probably born at Hever, the home of her father Sir Thomas Boleyn. After Anne's execution the house was seized by Henry and later given in 1540 to his fourth wife Anne of Cleves as part of the divorce settlement.

The excesses associated with the reign of the Tudors are best recalled at the Tower of London where so many people were imprisoned or executed. The protests, burnings and executions, which were among the repercussions of Henry's disastrous marriages and directly related to the progress made by Protestant reformers in Britain, have been remembered in other parts of the country besides London. A plaque on a wall at Norwich Castle commemorates the bravery of Robert Kett who led the unsuccessful Norfolk Rebellion of 1549 and at Bury St Edmunds a cross honours the memory of 17 Protestant martyrs who were executed in the town during the reign of Queen Mary I.

Henry VIII's break with the Church in Rome meant that Britain faced the very real threat of invasion for the first time since the Norman Conquest. France and the Holy Roman Empire had agreed to help the Pope; so Henry prepared for the possible threat of invasion by building a string of coastal forts from St Mawes in Cornwall to Hull on Humberside. The largest of these artillery forts

IN 1549 A.D. ROBERT KETT YEOMAN FARMER OF
WYMONDHAM WAS EXECUTED BY HANGING IN
THIS CASTLE AFTER THE DEFEAT OF THE NORFOLK
REBELLION OF WHICH HE WAS THE LEADER
IN 1949 A.D. FOUR HUNDRED YEARS LATER THIS
MEMORIAL WAS PLACED HERE BY THE CITIZENS
OF NORWICH IN REPARATION AND HONOUR TO
A NOTABLE AND COURAGEOUS LEADER IN THE
LONG STRUGGLE OF THE COMMON PEOPLE OF
ENGLAND TO ESCAPE FROM A SERVILE LIFE
INTO THE FREEDOM OF JUST CONDITIONS

was at Deal in Kent which was built between 1539 and 1540. It had a large circular keep and six wide, round bastions at a lower level. It was armed with guns mounted on wheels which could be moved from one gun port to another. They had a range of about 1½ miles.

The coastal fort at Tilbury played a prominent part during the threat from the Spanish Armada in 1588 when Queen Elizabeth addressed her troops there. 'I know I have the body of a weak and feeble woman but I have the heart and stomach of a king', she said. Little remains of Henry's fort, however, and the present fort was begun in 1670 to defend the Thames estuary against the Dutch.

IN LOVING MEMORY
OF THE
SEVENTEEN PROTESTANT MARTYRS
WHO FOR THEIR FAITHFUL TESTIMONY TO GOD'S TRUTH
DURING THE REIGN OF QUEEN MARY
SUFFERED DEATH IN THIS TOWN 1555-1558

TOP *Hever Castle, Kent.*

ABOVE LEFT *Plaque at Norwich Castle.*

LEFT *Inscription on a cross in Bury St Edmunds, Suffolk.*

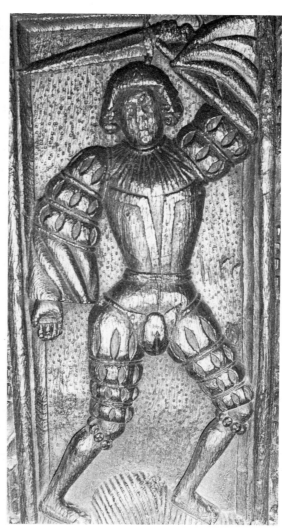

Early sixteenth-century bench ends at Altarnon in Cornwall showing FAR LEFT *a man with a cauldron*, LEFT *A man with a sword.*

BELOW *Tudor fort at Deal in Kent.*

Tudor Houses

The Tudor period saw the final transition from the fortified manor house of the fifteenth century to the elegant mansions of the Stuart and Georgian periods.

Cardinal Wolsey led the way with his magnificent palace of Hampton Court which had over 1000 rooms and about 500 servants to maintain it. When Wolsey fell from favour he gave Hampton Court to the King – a remarkable gift, not that it did Wolsey much good.

One of the finest of the great Tudor houses is at Longleat in Wiltshire, set amid magnificent grounds which were landscaped by 'Capability' Brown in the middle of the eighteenth century. Like Montacute House, one of its near neighbours, Longleat was designed on symmetrical lines – one of the characteristic features of Tudor design. It had a Great Hall like the manor houses and castles of the Middle Ages. At Montacute this was used only by the servants and was already beginning to resemble the entrance hall of today. Withdrawing rooms, parlours and the Great Chamber provided luxurious reception rooms for the owner and his family and their guests. The company withdrew to the Withdrawing Room after dinner; later it was simply known as the Drawing Room.

The most distinctive feature of the internal architecture of a Tudor mansion, however, was the Long Gallery which usually stretched right across the front of the house. At Longleat the Long Gallery is 90 feet long and at Montacute it is a massive 172 feet in length. Externally the most distinctive features of a Tudor mansion are the very tall brick chimneys and the large mullioned windows. Window glass began to be used extensively in the homes of the well-to-do in the Tudor period.

A particularly distinctive feature was the use of the upstairs oriel window resting on corbels. Features like this can be seen mirrored in the much simpler domestic architecture of the Tudor town or village such as the building in the photograph (right). Many town houses were built with upper storeys supported on protruding floor joists called jetties. This provided more room upstairs but had the disadvantage that in a narrow street the overhanging second and third storeys were so close to those on the opposite side of the street that people could even lean out and shake hands.

ABOVE *Longleat House in Wiltshire. The Tudor mansion and the gardens landscaped by 'Capability' Brown in the middle of the eighteenth century are shown.*

TOP *Montacute House, Somerset.*

ABOVE LEFT *Dutch gable at Montacute House with an oriel window on the left.*

ABOVE *Mullioned window at Montacute House.*

Tudor houses in Lavenham, Suffolk.

Tudor Shops

Tudor and mediaeval shops opened directly on to the street. The shopkeeper pulled down a wooden shutter in the early morning and this acted as a counter for the shop's wares. A relatively rare example of such a shop can be seen in Lavenham in Suffolk.

An impression of what the premises of a cloth finisher might have looked like in Tudor times is provided in a carved bench end at Spaxton in Somerset. Here the clothier is shown brushing a roll of woollen cloth lying on his counter, with the tools of his trade close at hand, including a comb and a pair of shears.

Street names today often provide a clue to the shops which could have been seen in a mediaeval town. Even in towns more renowned for their modern industries than their historical past, street names recall the Middle Ages such as Shambles Street in Barnsley where the butchers had their stalls. In mediaeval times the type of shop could be identified from the sign hanging above the shop such as a key, pair of scissors or a shoe. Shop signs can still be seen in some towns such as the pestle and mortar sign outside a chemist's shop in Rye in Sussex or the bristling pig outside a former brush shop in Kendal in Cumbria. Many museums have excellent collections of shop signs like these such as those to be seen in the Strangers Museum in Norwich.

Most towns and many large villages had a central market place such as the Saturday and Tuesday market places in King's Lynn in Norfolk. In many towns the market cross was stepped so that the market people could put their goods for sale on the steps below the cross.

More sophisticated market crosses were covered over for the benefit of customer and trader alike. At Chichester in Sussex, Bishop Edward Story erected a magnificent market cross in 1501 at the meeting place of the four main roads in the city. In some towns more substantial buildings

RIGHT *Sixteenth-century carved bench end at Spaxton in Somerset. The premises and tools of a cloth finisher are shown.*

Tudor shops in Lady Street, Lavenham, Suffolk.

ABOVE *Pestle and mortar sign above a chemist's shop in Rye, Sussex.*

BELOW *Sign above a former brush shop in Kendal, Cumbria.*

The marketplace in Lavenham in Suffolk showing the stepped market cross. The building on the right is believed to have been the toll house where the traders paid their tolls.

were later constructed such as the market hall in Ross-on-Wye in Herefordshire which was built in 1660–74.

Schools and Universities

The Tudor and Stuart periods were noteworthy for the foundation of many grammar schools, some of which have since been transformed into public schools and some into comprehensive schools. For instance the schools at Bedford, Christ's Hospital, King Edward's (Bath), King Edward's (Birmingham), King Edward's (Witley), Leeds Grammar, Shrewsbury and Tonbridge were all founded in either 1552 or 1553. Many were founded by wealthy merchants for the sons of local citizens.

The rules of many of these schools survive so it is possible to picture the life of one of Shakespeare's 'whining schoolboys'. The day began at 06.00 and went on to 17.00 – the pupils enjoying an unremitting diet of Latin, Greek, Hebrew, English Grammar and the Bible. Those who went to Market Harborough Grammar School (founded in 1613) would at least have had some relief from their studies, for the school was unusual in that it shared the same premises as the town's buttermarket which was held on the ground floor of the building!

Many of the colleges at Oxford and Cambridge were also founded in the mediaeval and Tudor periods, such as King's College, Cambridge, founded in 1441 – although its celebrated chapel was not completed until the reign of Henry VIII.

ABOVE *Market cross in Chichester in Sussex.*

BELOW *Seventeenth-century market hall at Ross-on-Wye in Herefordshire.*

LEFT *The early seventeenth-century grammar school at Market Harborough in Leicestershire.*

BELOW *The early seventeenth-century grammar school at Steyning in Sussex – now a comprehensive school.*

King's College Chapel, Cambridge.

Stuart Britain

The Stuart period lasted just over a hundred years, during which time there was civil war between King and Parliament, a serious rebellion in the West Country, the execution of a king (Charles I), the restoration of one of his sons as king (Charles II) and the expulsion of another son (James II).

For a period of eleven years there was no king at all and Britain was governed first by Parliament and then by a dictator, Oliver Cromwell, as Lord Protector of the Commonwealth.

The conflict between King and Parliament was not inevitable but it may have been a necessary stage in the transition from the rule of the last of the Tudors, a powerful autocratic monarch (Queen Elizabeth I), to the emergence of the first prime minister, Sir Robert Walpole, in the reign of the first of the Georges in the eighteenth century.

The Catholics expected James I, son of Mary Queen of Scots, to favour their cause when he came to the throne whilst the Puritans hoped the King would lean towards them instead. In practice both Catholics and Puritans were persecuted; so in 1620 a small group of Puritans left Plymouth in *The Mayflower* to start a new life in North America. Their departure point on the quayside at Plymouth is commemorated in a memorial and a datestone.

When the Puritans were later in the ascendant during the Commonwealth they left their mark on Britain in many ways, albeit negatively, since many church monuments can be seen which were disfigured or destroyed by Puritan soldiers during the Civil War and afterwards.

One of the blackest periods in Stuart history came with the aftermath of the Duke of Monmouth's rebellion against James II in 1685, when the notorious Judge Jeffreys presided at a series of brutal trials at which many of the rebels and suspected rebels were sentenced to execution, transportation, imprisonment or flogging.

An unusual relic from this time can be seen in the churchyard at Chedzoy in Somerset. Deep scores in the wall of the south transept may have been made by the rustic soldiers who joined the Duke of Monmouth's army and who are thought to have used the wall to sharpen their spears and knives before marching the $1\frac{1}{2}$ miles to the battlefield at Sedgemoor. There the raw and inexperienced army was crushed by James II's professional soldiers on 6 July 1685.

Statue of King Charles I in Trafalgar Square.

BELOW RIGHT *Mayflower Stone, Plymouth.*

ABOVE *Queen Elizabeth's Pocket Pistol at Dover, Kent.*

ABOVE RIGHT *Deep scores in the wall of Chedzoy Church in Somerset. They are believed to have been made by rebel soldiers before the battle of Sedgemoor in 1685.*

The Civil War

Most of the major battles of the Civil War have been commemorated by plaques or memorial stones. The obelisk at Naseby in Northamptonshire is probably the most significant, since it was here that the Parliamentary forces delivered the decisive blow.

It was nearly four years later that the King met his execution with bravery on a platform outside Banqueting House in Whitehall, an event recalled by a small plaque and a bust of Charles I.

Some of the guns and cannonballs which were used in the Civil War can still be seen in various parts of Britain. 'Queen Elizabeth's Pocket Pistol' is on display at Dover Castle. Although the gun was made in 1544 it was used by both the Royalist and Parliamentary armies in the Civil War since it was captured from the King in 1643 and recaptured the following year.

Numerous examples of battle damage alleged to have been caused by the two sides can be seen across the country, such as the bullet-ridden door of Blythburgh Church in Suffolk, the bullet holes in Siege House in Colchester or in the door of an almshouse in Barnstaple in Devon.

LEFT *Monument to the battle in 1645 at Naseby in Northamptonshire.*

ABOVE *Civil War bullet holes in the door of Penrose's Almshouses in Barnstaple in Devon.*

Pepys' England

Samuel Pepys' celebrated diary spans a period of less than ten years from the period just before the Restoration of Charles II in 1660 to a time at the end of that decade when his declining eyesight impelled him to end his daily journal. This remarkable record provides an incredibly detailed picture of the diarist's life and, through it, of everyday life in Stuart England in the 1660s.

On 15 November 1661 the coach he was travelling in couldn't manage the ascent of Fish Street Hill and he and his wife had to walk home with a link boy lighting the way ahead with a flaming torch. Pepys' England was changing. In his diary he describes drinking 'jocolatte' (chocolate) for the first time in November 1664 and also tea on 25 September 1660. 'I did send for a cup of tea of which I never had drank before.' Coffee houses were by then well in fashion and a plaque in the

Street sign in London.

Plaque and bust commemorating the execution of King Charles I in Whitehall in 1649.

Penrose's Almshouses in Barnstaple in Devon – founded in 1627.

City of London notes the position of London's first coffee house 'at the sign of Pasqua Rosee's Head 1652'.

In Tudor times beggars had been a problem, particularly after the Dissolution of the Monasteries. The nursery rhyme 'Hark! Hark! The dogs do bark' is believed to date from this time. Punitive laws against idle beggars were passed but at the same time some attempt was made to alleviate genuine poverty for those unable to help themselves. In the seventeenth century, in particular, many almshouses were founded to provide homes for the sick, infirm and aged.

The Plague

Samuel Pepys kept up his diary during the plague of 1665–6. Unlike many other Londoners he did not desert the city. He mentioned the 'sicknesse' for the first time on 30 April 1665 and five weeks later on 7 June wrote 'This day, much against my will, I did in Drury Lane see two or three houses marked with a red cross upon the doors, and "Lord have mercy upon us!" writ there.'

Very little remains in London today to recall the days when the plague was killing at least 1000 people every day at its peak. Undoubtedly the great fire of 1666 destroyed much that would have been of macabre interest. For that one must travel to Eyam in Derbyshire where numerous relics recall the effect which the plague had on a small northern village.

At the beginning of September 1665 a tailor called George Vicars opened a parcel of clothes which had arrived from plague-ridden London. The next day he started to shiver and on 7 September was dead. The epidemic quickly spread but the vicar, the Reverend William Mompesson persuaded the villagers to stay rather than run the risk of spreading it further throughout the country. As a result over 250 of the 350 villagers died, including the vicar's wife Catherine. Goods were brought to the edge of Eyam by people from neighbouring villages. They received payment from coins left in vinegar in holes in stones on the village boundary. Plague stones like these can be seen in other towns as well, such as in Derby and in Bury St Edmunds.

TOP *Tomb of Catherine Mompesson in Eyam churchyard, Derbyshire.*

ABOVE *The Plague Stone in Bury St Edmunds, Suffolk.*

RIGHT *Sign outside Plague Cottages in Eyam.*

The Great Fire of London

Just after midnight on 1 September 1666 a fire began to burn in Thomas Farriner's bakery in Pudding Lane near London Bridge. It was soon fanned by the wind, with the result that the fire spread to other houses in Pudding Lane and ultimately right across the City. For five days London burned. John Evelyn, another seventeenth-century diarist, described 'the noise and crackling and thunder' of the fire which, he said, was like 'a hideous storm; and the air all about so hot and inflamed that at the last one was not able to approach it.'

The old cathedral of St Paul's was destroyed, together with 88 other churches and 13 200 houses. This appalling disaster had one good effect, however, since it did destroy the breeding grounds for the plague.

Afterwards wealthy Londoners were able to insure against fire. Insurance companies were founded and equipped with their own fire engines. They fought only the fires of their policy holders, so firemarks were issued to be attached to the insured properties, in order to make certain that the private fire brigades did not waste time putting out fires which were not their responsibility!

LEFT *The monument which commemorates the Great Fire of London – standing 202 feet high and exactly 202 feet away from the house in Pudding Lane where the fire began.*

ABOVE *Street sign in London.*

Firemark on a building in Saffron Walden in Essex. The sun was the mark used by the Sun Fire Office.

Stuart Architecture

St Paul's Cathedral.

Sir Christopher Wren was one of the architects who helped to restore the city and build many of its fine new churches. His masterpiece was St Paul's Cathedral, of course, which he began in 1675 and saw completed in 1711 when he was 79 years of age. Other well-known buildings which he helped to design include the Sheldonian Theatre and Ashmolean Museum in Oxford, extensions to Hampton Court, the Greenwich Observatory and parts of Westminster Abbey.

Domestic buildings from the Stuart and Queen Anne periods are very distinctive. They often have a hipped roof (one with a pitched roof on all four sides), symmetrical windows (often with the ground floor windows slightly longer than those on the first floor), a central pediment and quoins at the corners.

Regional Styles of Building

Decorated plasterwork, called pargetting, is a characteristic feature of many Stuart houses in East Anglia. Some of these designs are embossed and stand proud of the plaster like that of the Ancient House in Ipswich. Others have incised patterns which are less susceptible to weathering.

Late Stuart house at Nunney in Somerset.

Late seventeenth-century pargetting on the Ancient House in Ipswich.

Britain has a rich heritage of distinctive building styles like this – only a selected few of which can be shown here. Some of these styles are decorative like pargetting and hung tiles, others derive their distinction from the character of the building material such as limestone in the Cotswolds and cob and thatch in Dorset and Devon. Other styles of building are mainly structural, such as the cruck-framed timber houses of Herefordshire and the west or the box-framed 'Wealden' houses of Kent and Sussex and other eastern counties.

Flint wall in Saffron Walden, Essex, consisting of squared stone to form the edges and corners and a mixture of whole flints and split flints embedded in mortar.

Crow-stepped gables on a stone house in St Andrews, Fifeshire. Note the stone forestairs giving outside access to the first floor of the house.

BELOW *Cotswold limestone houses in Chipping Campden in Gloucestershire.*

ABOVE LEFT *Cob and thatch cottages in Tolpuddle, Dorset. Cob was a mixture of clay, sand and straw (and sometimes animal hair).*

BELOW LEFT *The half-timbered fifteenth-century Wealden farmhouse of Smallhythe Place near Tenterden in Kent – similar in construction to the house shown on page 47 which has been re-erected at Singleton.*

Industry

The beginnings of the industrial revolution can be seen in the seventeenth century. Coal production increased twelve-fold between 1550 and 1690, from 200 000 tonnes a year to 2 500 000 tonnes. A tax on sea-cole, so-called because it was taken by sea from the Tyne to London, helped to finance the rebuilding of St Paul's Cathedral.

It was also a time of experiment. Quite apart from the discoveries of Isaac Newton and William Harvey there were striking new inventions such as Thomas Newcomen's atmospheric steam engine of 1698 and Abraham Darby's successful use of coke to smelt iron ore in the first decade of the eighteenth century.

The iron industry was still firmly based on charcoal-burning furnaces and forges but supplies of suitable timber were running out. At the start of the seventeenth century the Weald of Kent and Sussex resounded with the sounds of heavy industry. Cowden hammerpond, like the pond behind Wortley Forge in Yorkshire, was one of many which impounded water to be fed into a goit or

TOP *Heavy helve hammer operated by a cam on the waterwheel – at Top Forge, Wortley near Sheffield.*

LEFT *Cowden hammerpond in Kent.*

ABOVE *London street sign near St Paul's Cathedral.*

narrow channel, to turn a waterwheel which powered the bellows in a furnace room and the heavy hammers in a forge.

Georgian Britain

For many people the word 'Georgian' evokes a time of matchless elegance, exquisite manners, and distinctive culture. Yet it was also a time of squalid slums, tyrannical laws and barbaric punishments; of colonial expansion and conquest and a period of rapid technological change in agriculture, industry and transport. Strikingly original solutions were made to the technical (but not the social) problems presented by a rapidly growing industry and a developing agriculture.

The Britain of George Frideric Handel, Jane Austen, Dr Johnson, Thomas Gainsborough, Richard Arkwright, James Watt and 'Turnip'

The Pantiles in Royal Tunbridge Wells, Kent.

Townshend was also a Britain where young children were hanged in public for stealing a pittance, where people could starve or drink themselves to death; a Britain where disease, crime and poverty were endemic.

Because the great mansions and town houses are the most widespread, permanent and distinctive features of this Georgian inheritance, it is easy to see why 'Georgian' tends to be synonymous with style and elegance rather than with industrial change, poverty, cruelty or oppression.

The great figures of the eighteenth and early nineteenth centuries stand comparison with those of any other age. It is arguable, that in relation to a total British population of approximately 6 500 000 in 1750, the Georgian period produced more than its expected share of men and women of outstanding genius. All the more remarkable that this was achieved at a time when very few people went to school, let alone university.

Statues, monuments, plaques and even houses celebrate and commemorate the achievements of Georgians such as Thomas Gainsborough in Sudbury in Suffolk, Dr Johnson in Fleet Street and General Wolfe at Westerham in Kent.

The less acceptable face of Georgian Britain is not so prominent.

The harsh reality of Georgian and Regency times can be recalled at Tyburn Way and Marble Arch where London's public executions took place on Tyburn Tree (the popular name for the gallows). It is evident, too, in the relics of the aftermath of the ill-fated Stuart rebellions of 1715 and 1745. The battle of Culloden was fought on the moors to the south of Inverness on 16 April 1746. It lasted 40 minutes, the repercussions much longer. The Hanoverian troops under 'Butcher' Cumberland, second son of King George II, pursued the fleeing Highlanders and killed many of them in cold blood. A policy of repression in the Scottish Highlands led eventually to the destruction of the clan system and ultimately to widespread depopulation. Absentee landlords found it more profitable to rear sheep; so many families were evicted to make way for sheep farmers. Derelict crofts can still be seen in the Highlands, testifying not only to the evictions of the early nineteenth century but to the continuing depopulation ever since.

The brutality of the period may also be evoked

Statue of James Watt in the centre of Leeds.

FAR RIGHT *Statue of Captain Cook near Admiralty Arch in London.*

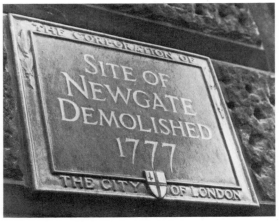

ABOVE *Plaque marking the spot where Newgate Prison used to stand in London – from which so many people were taken in the cart to the gallows at Tyburn.*

LEFT *Memorial stone on Culloden Moor, marking the spot where Alexander MacGillivray fell during the battle.*

BELOW LEFT *Derelict cottage at the side of Destitution Road near Ullapool in Ross and Cromarty. The road got its name because it was built to alleviate hardship during the 1851 famine.*

in Tolpuddle in Dorset although it is hard to reconcile this charming village (see page 76) with the trial of the six farmworkers whose attempt to form a trade union was rewarded with a brutal sentence of transportation in 1834. But a stark reminder of those times may even now deter potential vandals on the bridge at Sturminster Newton a few miles away!

The Napoleonic Wars

It is an interesting but perhaps inevitable feature of the Kent coastline, that within the space of a few miles it is possible to see important coastal fortifications, ranging from those of the Romans at Richborough, the Normans at Dover and the Tudors at Deal to those of the Georgians at Hythe.

The Georgian coastal defences consisted of a line of circular forts, built of brick, called Martello Towers after a fort in northern Corsica (the Torre della Mortella) which had defied and impressed the British navy on 7 February 1794. Over 100 of these artillery forts were erected between 1805 and 1812 at sites stretching from Suffolk to Sussex. Remains of 43 of these towers can be seen today.

Monuments to the men who died in these wars are relatively rare although many churches have memorials to the individual soldiers and sailors who died in the many battles of this period. An unusual monument to the war is passed every day by thousands of motorists using the A1 near Peterborough. The obelisk which stands at Norman Cross carries the inscription:

> To the memory of one thousand seven hundred and seventy soldiers and sailors natives or allies of France taken prisoners of war during the Republican and Napoleonic Wars with Great Britain AD 1793–1814 who died in the military depot at Norman Cross which formerly stood near this spot.

If the contribution of the soldiers whom Wellington described as 'the scum of the earth' is barely commemorated, there can be no complaint of a shortage of monuments to the two men who engineered the two greatest victories.

Wellington not only bestrides his horse outside the Royal Exchange and at Hyde Park Corner in London, he and his victories are also commemor-

Memorial at Norman Cross, Cambridgeshire.

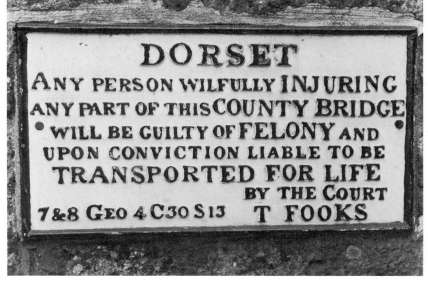

Warning notice on a bridge at Sturminster Newton, Dorset.

BELOW *Martello tower at Seaford, Sussex.*

BOTTOM *The Duke of Wellington's town residence of Apsley House at Hyde Park Corner. It was sometimes known simply as No. 1 London.*

Statue of the Duke of Wellington at Hyde Park Corner.

BELOW *Nelson's Column in Trafalgar Square.*

BELOW RIGHT *Relief depicting the battle of Trafalgar on a panel at the base of Nelson's Column.*

ated at Waterloo Station, Wellington College, Waterloo Place, Wellington in New Zealand and innumerable Wellington streets, to say nothing of wellington boots and a tree (*Wellingtonia*).

Nelson, too, is remembered – most notably in Trafalgar Square where scenes of his victory are shown in panels at the base of the Column and also in place names such as Nelson in Lancashire, Nelson Street in King's Lynn and countless Nelson inns.

Georgian Mansions

The great mansions of Georgian Britain owed their inspiration, in the main, to the ideas of the architects of the Classical era. Many architects were influenced by the sixteenth-century Italian architect Palladio whose *Book of Architecture* was based on the Classical designs of ancient Rome. Houses designed on these lines, like Holkham Hall in Norfolk, are therefore said to be Palladian in style.

The Classical influence can be seen in the overall plan of many Georgian houses and in the use of columns conforming to the Classical orders such as Doric, Ionic, Corinthian and Tuscan. Six Corinthian columns form the front of the portico at Holkham and they support the pediment (triangular gable) above.

The influence of ancient Greece and Rome can also be seen in other features such as the Temple of Concord, erected in 1791 in the grounds of Audley End house in Essex, and in the terracotta frieze encircling the rotunda at Ickworth House in Suffolk which depicts scenes from Homer.

Ickworth House was started in 1795 and is unusual in that its dominant feature is a huge oval rotunda. It is not unique, however, for a circular mansion had earlier been built on Belle Isle at Bowness-on-Windermere in the Lake District. The gardens of Ickworth House, like those of many other great Georgian mansions including Holkham Hall, were landscaped by 'Capability' Brown. Some wealthy landowners even pulled down cottages and hamlets in order to improve the view from their windows.

Possibly the most striking and certainly the most unusual Georgian mansion in Britain is the Royal Pavilion in Brighton whose appearance today was designed by John Nash. It was based on an earlier building which had already been altered and considerably enlarged for the Prince Regent. It was erected between 1815 and 1822.

Holkham Hall, Norfolk.

Whereas the great Georgian mansions are almost invariably set amid superbly landscaped grounds the Royal Pavilion is in the centre of Brighton and within a few hundred yards of the sea. Above all it was based on the 'Mahometan architecture of Hindostan' and its domes and minarets are clearly derived from the mosques of the Indian sub-continent.

RIGHT *Temple of Concord, Audley End, Essex.*

BELOW *Terracotta frieze at Ickworth House near Bury St Edmunds, Suffolk.*

Ickworth House.

with its three openings – a tall round-arched frame in the centre and two smaller square-topped windows at the sides. Balustrades are commonly found at the base of these windows and also above the cornices at roof level.

Many town houses were built as terraces, crescents or even in a complete circle or circus. They often had basement kitchens with a coal cellar adjoining. External access to the coal cellar was often through a hole in the pavement. The basement windows were often half above and half below street level. The *area* in front of the basement was protected by iron railings, which extended from the entrance steps of one house to those of its neighbour.

In the Regency period (early nineteenth century) many houses were built with bow windows and decorative wrought ironwork for railings, gates and balconies.

This rich heritage of Georgian and Regency

The Royal Pavilion, Brighton.

Georgian Architecture

A symmetrical façade and dentillations in the cornice, projecting just below roof level, are two characteristic features of many Georgian buildings, such as the White Hart Hotel in Lewes in Sussex and the elegant avenue of Southernhay West in Exeter. The immediate impression is one of tall perpendicular buildings with flat roofs. This is because the cornice was often deliberately over-emphasized in order to obscure the pitch of the roof behind. By contrast the hipped roof was the most prominent feature of domestic buildings of the Queen Anne period which preceded it.

Other characteristics of the Georgian style include the highly distinctive doorway with a pediment and a portico, and also the Venetian window

building reflects the upsurge in wealth which came with improvements in agriculture and industry and with the activities of fortune hunters in the burgeoning empire abroad.

Georgian Towns

Many other buildings date back to the Georgian and Regency periods and reflect the polarity between affluence and poverty at that time. Bath is the outstanding example of a sophisticated and fashionable Georgian town with the Royal Crescent, Pump Room, Assembly Rooms and Pulteney Bridge with its row of elegant shops.

A number of delightful Georgian and Regency

TOP *Southernhay West, Exeter.*

ABOVE *Venetian window with a balustrade at its base and an urn in a wall niche on the right – the eighteenth-century Market Cross in Bury St Edmunds, Suffolk.*

BELOW *Wrought ironwork at Rydal Hall in Cumbria.*

TOP *White Hart Hotel in Lewes, Sussex.*

ABOVE *Georgian doorway in Stokesley in north Yorkshire.*

theatres have been preserved in different parts of the country, such as those at Richmond in north Yorkshire, Bury St Edmunds in Suffolk and Stamford in Lincolnshire. Assembly Rooms, too, where the Georgian *beau monde* could meet and dance are not uncommon – although the centre of a

Balustrade at Rydal Hall.

modern industrial city like Newcastle-upon-Tyne is perhaps unexpected.

Because Georgian and Regency shops, with their small window panes and bow windows, are so captivating in appearance it is small wonder that quite a number survive, like those shown here in Kent. A particularly elegant row of shops can be seen in Woburn Walk in London whilst Burlington Arcade in the West End is an outstanding example of a Regency shopping precinct, built between 1815 and 1819.

It is less easy to find some evidence or inkling of the appalling living conditions in which the vast majority of people lived, such as the slums shown so realistically in Hogarth's paintings and engravings. Most of these were pulled down long ago, but in the old quarter of Edinburgh it is still possible to see the relatively rare sight of seventeenth-century tenement buildings – ordinary homes which would have been teeming with people in Georgian times.

Workhouse buildings, erected to house the local paupers, can also be seen which date from this period. These are often as gloomy and as forbidding today as they must have been then, but there are exceptions. An impressive workhouse with a central pediment can be seen at Stowmarket in Suffolk. It was completed in 1781. Conditions inside the workhouse were nothing like as palatial as the external appearance of this building might suggest. In the workhouse cemetery close by numbers are marked on the gravestones rather than names.

Crime flourished in the Georgian town despite

Assembly Rooms dating from 1776 in Newcastle-upon-Tyne.

BELOW *Georgian theatre in Stamford, Lincolnshire.*

Weatherboarded Georgian shops at Tenterden in Kent.

draconian laws. It is not surprising, therefore, to find that most towns and large villages had a cage or lock-up. The circular lock-up at Castle Cary in Somerset, which was built in 1779, is only seven feet in diameter and about ten feet high. One of its two iron ventilation grilles can be seen above the doorway shown in the photograph.

Lock-up (or cage) at Castle Cary, Somerset.

LEFT *Seventeenth-century tenements in Edinburgh.*

Workhouse in Stowmarket, Suffolk.

Everyday Life

Some indication of the everyday life of people in Georgian Britain can occasionally be evoked by features which have long been obsolete. Evidence of Georgian commerce and trade, for example, can be seen in a few rare instances such as at Dunkeld in Perthshire where an eighteenth-century ell measure is attached to the wall of a building in the town centre. The ell was a measure of length (about 37 inches in Scotland) and best remembered for the non-metric proverb 'give him an inch and he'll take an ell'.

In Barnstaple, in Devon, an Exchange for use by merchants and shipowners was built close to the river in the early eighteenth century. When the merchants put their money down on the Tome Stone this clinched the deal. A similar stone in Bristol was called the 'nail' – hence the phrase 'paying on the nail'.

The cement-rendered cone near Dallington in Sussex is a folly. It was erected by a local squire, Mad Jack Fuller, in the early nineteenth century. Its resemblance to the top of a church spire is deliberate. Jack Fuller lost a wager that Dallington

RIGHT *Ell measure in Dunkeld, Perthshire.*

BELOW *Tome Stone in Barnstaple, Devon.*

church spire could be seen from the grounds of his house, so he built this 'sugar loaf', as it is called, to remedy matters!

For most people the only way of travelling efficiently through a town was on horseback. In the country it is quite common to see mounting blocks outside a church or inn. In a major city it is relatively rare – hence the special interest in this mounting block in Waterloo Place in the centre of London which was erected, so it is said, at the suggestion of the Duke of Wellington.

In Norwich a plaque on a wall recalls the spot where a sedan chair could be hired in the 1800s. The sedan chair was a particularly useful form of transport in the Georgian town, since it could be carried down narrow passages as well as across wide streets.

Travel at night in the eighteenth century was hazardous. There were some oil lamps in the large streets but most were in the dark. The wealthy got a servant or a link boy to light the way ahead with

TOP *Mad Jack Fuller's folly at Dallington in Sussex.*

ABOVE *Plaque on a wall in the centre of Norwich.*

ABOVE LEFT *Mounting block in Waterloo Place, London.*

LEFT *Link extinguisher (sometimes called a snuffer or torch extinguisher) outside a house in Queen Anne's Gate, London.*

89

a flaming torch, called a link. This is why one or two houses in London still have a link extinguisher at the side of the front door. It was used to snuff out the flames on arriving back home.

Enclosed fields near Penistone, south Yorkshire

BOTTOM *Georgian farmhouse at Milbourne near Newcastle-upon-Tyne.*

The Agricultural Revolution

Striking changes altered the appearance of the countryside in the eighteenth and nineteenth centuries. The huge open fields were enclosed by newly planted hedges, wooden fences and stone walls. It is an ironic commentary on the modern farmer's grubbing out of hedges, that in the process it is giving the countryside a mediaeval look once more!

When the land was farmed in common and a farmer had many strips in a number of widely scattered fields, it made sense to have the cottage or farmhouse in the centre of the village. When the land was redistributed as compact parcels of land, it meant that farmers could build their farmhouses and farm buildings on their own property close to their fields. This is why so many farmhouses date back to Georgian times and the early Victorian period when most of the enclosures took place.

The only surviving example of the open-field system is the village of Laxton in Nottinghamshire where the farmers still cultivate the land in strips. The most surprising feature of the village today is the fact that most of the farmhouses are situated on either side of the long main street.

The farming improvements of the eighteenth and nineteenth centuries included new crop rota-

tions, use of manures and fertilizers, selective breeding of animals and the reclamation of poor land. Windmills and windpumps were used to drain marshland whilst many farmers planted trees on poorer sandy land.

Many farm buildings in use today date back to the eighteenth and nineteenth centuries, if not earlier. Only rarely, however, is it still possible to see barns standing on staddle stones to let the air circulate underneath, at the same time inhibiting all but the most agile of rats. The gin gang house (or horse walk) is rather more common, especially in north-eastern England and in Fifeshire. This was a circular or polygonal building in which horses were walked round and round in shafts which turned a central wheel, providing power to operate machinery such as a thrashing machine. When steam replaced horse power the farmer had to build a boiler house and chimney stack and these can sometimes be seen nearby as well.

The industrialization of farming had other forerunners such as the circular oast houses which were used for drying hops in the middle of the nineteenth century and which are mainly obsolete today. The cowl on the top was turned by the wind and this helped to maximize the draught.

Village Life

Few houses in the eighteenth century had their own private water supply, so the pump or well was one of the most important public amenities in a village. At Little Walsingham, in Norfolk, the octagonal conduit has a conical roof which provided a shelter over the village water supply. The Walsingham conduit also acted as a lock-up and the cresset or fire basket on top was used to hold a flaming torch or beacon.

TOP *The open field village of Laxton, Nottinghamshire.*

ABOVE *Large granary standing on staddle stones at the Weald and Downland Open Air Museum at Singleton, Sussex. It was built in c. 1731 and originally stood at Littlehampton in Sussex.*

The amenities in most villages were limited, as they were in the towns. At Papworth St Agnes in Cambridgeshire a rare survival from the past can be seen in the village bakehouse which dates from the nineteenth century. Charles Dickens described town children 'dancing for very joy' in the street as they surrounded a small beef joint which had been cooked in the oven in a baker's shop nearby. Few people had their own ovens (and so rarely ate meat) that it was worth their while to pay the baker for the privilege of using an oven when the need arose. Here at Papworth St Agnes the villagers shared a communal bakehouse in the centre of the village.

Villages were more self-contained in the eighteenth century than they are today. For one thing there were many more shops then, since the absence of cheap public transport and the high cost of private transport meant that most ordinary people had to purchase the bulk of their food, clothes and other domestic requirements within walking distances of their homes. Markets were very important to them and so too were the village shops. Most of these shops closed many years ago but old shop premises can often be detected where there are houses in the centre of the village with a large bow window but no corresponding windows above or at either side.

Many villages still retain the green, together with some of the features which would have been seen there in the eighteenth and early nineteenth centuries, such as a Gossip Tree where the villagers talked, the stocks, the pound where stray animals were impounded by the pindar and the village pond which enabled travellers to water their beasts.

Gin gang house, complete with horse wheel and chimney, at the North of England Open Air Museum at Beamish, County Durham.

BELOW *Oast houses at Ightham in Kent.*

Little Walsingham, Norfolk.

BELOW LEFT *Conduit and cresset at Little Walsingham.*

The communal bakehouse at Papworth St Agnes, Cambridgeshire.

Covered market cross in Alston, Cumbria, dating from 1765.

TOP *Village green and pond at Finchingfield in Essex.*

ABOVE *Bow-fronted shop in Alfriston, Sussex.*

The Industrial Revolution

The industrial revolution was really a period of evolution rather than a time of dramatic and sudden change. The seeds of industrialization had been sown in earlier centuries, but it was in the eighteenth century that the pace of industrial development quickened.

In the early eighteenth century the domestic character of many of Britain's industries can be recalled in carvings such as those on the tombstone of Jonathan Parker, a workman whose tools of trade can be seen in the churchyard in Saffron Walden in Essex.

At the start of the eighteenth century the wool industry was still a domestic industry carried out by spinners and weavers who worked in their own homes. They worked upstairs in rooms with long windows because they needed as much light as possible in order to extend the working day from dawn to dusk. Weavers' cottages, like these, are easily identified and can be seen in most areas where there was a flourishing cloth industry in the past. Many date from the early nineteenth century, for the transition from a domestic craft to a factory-based industry took time. Weavers' houses can even be seen in central London in the Spitalfields district near Liverpool Street Station. Street names also provide a clue to the existence of a former cloth industry. The cloth was stretched out on tenters to dry (hence the phrase 'on tenter-hooks') and holes made by tenterhooks can be clearly seen in the rolls of cloth depicted in the Tudor bench end carving shown on page 66.

The first application of power to the textile industry came with the use of the waterwheel. Richard Arkwright built the first water-powered textile mill at Cromford in Derbyshire in about 1771. This was the world's first factory for spinning cotton and it used Arkwright's spinning frame. It proved so successful and profitable that soon many other textile mills were built in Lancashire, Derbyshire and Yorkshire.

Water power eventually gave way to steam but the waterwheel continued to be a useful source of power for many industrial processes. The waterwheel at Kilhope in County Durham was used to power the rollers which crushed lead ore when it was washed.

The coal mining industry developed rapidly in the eighteenth century as the demand for coal rose with the invention of the steam engine. Remains of early bell pits can be seen near Wakefield in Yorkshire. Coal was converted to coke and used by Abraham Darby at Coalbrookdale to smelt iron ore in the early years of the eighteenth century. The more efficient production of iron enabled castings to be made and facilitated the manufacture of machinery and the steam engine.

The pioneers of steam were Thomas Newcomen and James Watt. A rare example of a Newcomen steam engine, dating from 1787, can be seen at the Elsecar colliery near Barnsley.

Georgian and early-Victorian factory workers and coal miners worked long hours in difficult conditions for small wages. A poignant reminder

TOP *Mason's tombstone in the churchyard at Saffron Walden in Essex.*

ABOVE *Street sign in Spitalfields, London.*

Early nineteenth-century weavers' cottages in Thurlstone, south Yorkshire.

of the shameful use of child labour in industry in the early years of the nineteenth century can be seen in the churchyard at Silkstone near Barnsley in south Yorkshire. A soot-begrimed monument records the names of the 26 victims who included Sarah Newton aged eight years, Sarah Jukes aged ten and Ann Moss aged nine. Heavy rain caused the hillside pit to flood in July 1838. On Kendray Hill, a few miles away in Barnsley, another monument is dedicated to the members of a rescuing party who were killed by a second explosion after searching through the Oaks Colliery workings to see if any of about 350 miners there were still alive after the first explosion in 1866.

Many other remains of the industrial revolution can be seen in Britain. Remains of old kilns, factories, industrial processes and the artefacts of industry, which were virtually ignored 25 years ago, are now being lovingly restored and preserved by industrial archaeologists. Museums of our industrial heritage proliferate and testify to general interest in this once-neglected aspect of our living history.

Richard Arkwright's cotton mill on the banks of the river Derwent at Cromford in Derbyshire.

RIGHT *Waterwheel and lead mill at Kilhope, County Durham. The wheel is about 34 feet in diameter.*

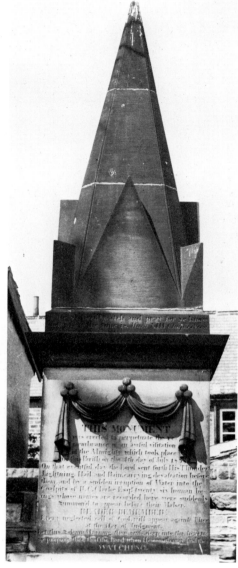

Newcomen pumping engine at Elsecar Colliery, near Barnsley.

BELOW *Nineteenth-century colliery at Beamish in County Durham. Here at the North of England Open Air Museum it is possible to visit pit workings, inspect the colliery and see replicas of miners' cottages.*

Monument in Silkstone churchyard, south Yorkshire to the victims of a coal-mining disaster in 1838.

Remains of a derelict kiln at Tilberthwaite in the Lake District.

Remains of a barge which was once used to carry sand on the Bude Canal in Cornwall. It was in use about 100 years ago and stands on the towpath today as a reminder of the canal's former importance.

Canals

The rapid development of heavy industry in the eighteenth century created a transportation problem, for although heavy raw materials were relatively cheap at their source, they were very expensive to transport by road. The solution, to take them by canal, changed the map of Britain. A horse could pull 500 bales of wool loaded on a canal barge compared to two bales when used as a pack horse.

For a period of about 80 years, from 1760 to 1840, thousands of miles of canal were constructed before the railways effectively killed them off. The first important canal was James Brindley's Bridgewater Canal completed in 1761 and used to carry coal from Worsley Colliery to Manchester.

It was an unqualified success, much admired by other civil engineers and more important, it halved the cost of carrying the coal from the pit to the city. Many factories were built on the banks of the new canals. The canal network linked the major industrial centres and the cities and provided the answer to the problem the manufacturers and other industrialists had been seeking to resolve.

Canal-side mill in Huddersfield, west Yorkshire.

Turnpike Roads

Roads at the beginning of the eighteenth century were generally in very poor condition. Daniel Defoe, Celia Fiennes and other travellers complained about ruts, potholes and mud. Each town or village was then responsible for the maintenance of the roads within its boundaries. Some

BELOW *Eighteenth-century milestone near Amesbury in Wiltshire.*

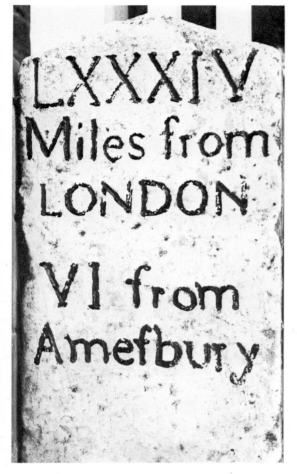

ABOVE *Narrow packhorse bridge near Penistone, south Yorkshire.*

BELOW *Carving on the tombstone of John Catchpole, a carrier, who died in 1787 at Palgrave in Suffolk. The inscription below this depiction of an eighteenth-century stage waggon reads:*

My horses has done Running
My Waggon is decay'd
And now in the Dust my Body is lay'd
My whip is worn out and my work it is done
And now I'm brought here to my last home

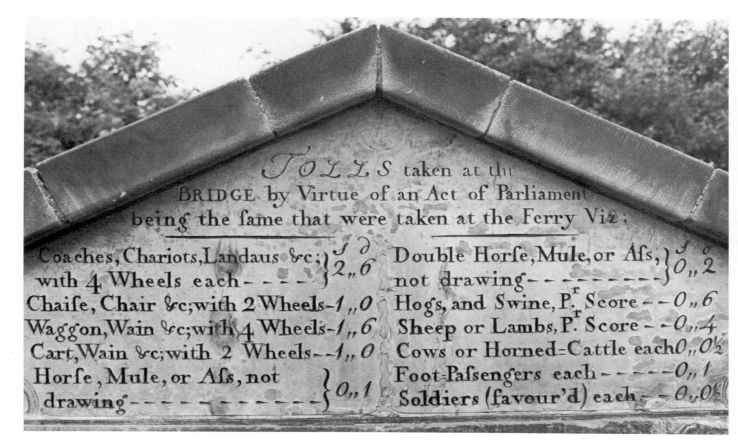

TOLLS taken at the
BRIDGE by Virtue of an Act of Parliament
being the same that were taken at the Ferry Viz:

	s	d		s	d
Coaches, Chariots, Landaus &c; with 4 Wheels each	2	6	Double Horse, Mule, or Afs, not drawing	0	2
Chaife, Chair &c; with 2 Wheels	1	0	Hogs, and Swine, Pr Score	0	6
Waggon, Wain &c; with 4 Wheels	1	6	Sheep or Lambs, Pr Score	0	4
Cart, Wain &c; with 2 Wheels	1	0	Cows or Horned=Cattle each	0	0½
Horse, Mule, or Afs, not drawing	0	1	Foot-Paffengers each	0	1
			Soldiers (favour'd) each	0	0½

Tollboard at Cavendish Bridge in Leicestershire.

Tollhouse at Great Whelnetham in Suffolk.

roads were in good condition but most were 'rough, middling' as one traveller put it.

The main forms of road transport reflected the poor road conditions. Packhorses were used to transport many goods, such as bales of wool (see page 59). Packhorse bridges which were only wide enough for one packhorse at a time took the packhorse routes across the rivers. Sometimes these trackways were paved like the raised 'causey' or causeway at Bradley in Huddersfield.

The other form of heavy transport for goods was the stage waggon. When a Suffolk carrier died in 1787 a carving of his stage waggon was made at the head of his tombstone. These cumbersome vehicles had large wide wheels to make them roadworthy on the rutted tracks which passed for highways in some parts of the country.

The roads improved beyond all recognition during the eighteenth and early nineteenth centuries. In the 1740s it took a stage coach about 12 days to travel from London to Edinburgh. By 1830 the total journey time by fast mail coach was 46 hours.

A sensational improvement like this was only possible because the turnpike trusts had provided Britain with the best roads it had had since the time of the Romans. In the early years of the nineteenth century, the work of skilled road engineers like Thomas Telford and John Loudon McAdam so improved road surfaces that mail coaches could be forced along at speeds that would have been suicidal in the first half of the eighteenth century.

The turnpike trusts were empowered by Parliament to charge tolls which would be used to maintain the roads they erected. The trusts were usually composed of local gentlemen and business people. When a new section of turnpike road was completed a barrier was erected across the entrance, with a tollgate and a small tollgate house for the tollkeeper. The barrier or bar was the actual turnpike rather than the road. One of the few remaining turnpike barriers can be seen at Hunters Bar near the centre of Sheffield. Tollboards can still be seen occasionally and tollhouses are quite common. They can be recognized from their distinctive appearance – usually built with six or eight sides so that the tollkeeper could keep a watch for traffic from every part of his house.

Coaching Inns

The golden age of coaching was in the 1820s when hundreds of coaches left London every day for towns throughout Britain. Most of the coaches had names which distinguished them from their rivals. At Stockport you could catch the *Jolly Potter* and the *Lord Nelson* whilst in nearby Oldham you could travel on the *Doctor*, *Morning Star* or *Wellington* for instance. There was considerable rivalry between the companies who operated the coaches. At Lancaster you could go to the King's Arms to catch *The New Times* at 11.30 a.m. or to Old Sir Simon's at the same time to catch *The Invincible*. Both coaches were en route to Carlisle and Edinburgh.

Unfortunately in the same decade the world's first passenger railway train made its maiden journey. Within 20 years the golden age was over although railway passengers still had the pleasure of travelling in railway carriages which resembled stage coaches.

The first mail coach services began in 1784 and, together with the improving stage coach services, transformed road travel in Britain. It was now possible for the well-to-do, who alone could afford to travel this way, to travel the length and breadth of Britain in relative comfort.

Most country market towns have at least one coaching inn today. Many face on to the main street with a porte cochere – an arched entrance – in the centre of the inn building through which the stage coach was driven to the galleried court-

Hunters Bar, Sheffield.

yard behind where the horses were changed. The George Hotel at Stamford, one of the greatest of these coaching inns, had two waiting rooms for passengers, one for those travelling north to York and another for passengers travelling south to London.

The Norfolk Arms in Arundel, Sussex – an eighteenth-century coaching inn with a central porte cochere.

Galleried courtyard of the Eagle Inn, Cambridge.

Signs outside the former waiting rooms for stage coach and mail coach passengers in the George Hotel in Stamford, Lincolnshire.

Victorian and Edwardian Britain

Diamond Jubilee (1897) plaque on the gables of a house in Hoylandswaine, south Yorkshire.

BOTTOM *Prince Albert depicted on the Clock Tower in the centre of Brighton.*

The four Georges had been generally despised; so when Victoria succeeded her uncle, William IV, in 1837 at the age of 18, she came to the throne at a time when the reputation of the monarchy was low. When she died in 1901 the nation mourned and people talked of the passing of an era (her death nearly coincided with the beginning of the new century). Queen Victoria laid the foundation for the new conception of the monarchy in the twentieth century, even though her own contribution to government was hardly distinguished and rarely impartial.

Her reign was commemorated so widely that it is virtually impossible to escape seeing a Victoria Street or a Victoria Inn. Images of the Queen range from statues to plaques, such as the Diamond Jubilee plate affixed to the gables of a house in Hoylandswaine in south Yorkshire. In one sense the celebration of the Queen was symbolic since it was during her reign that Britain and the British Empire reached the zenith of its political and economic importance.

Comparisons between the year of Queen Victoria's accession in 1837 and that of her death in 1901 show striking changes. Horse buses and sailing ships at the start of her reign had become motor buses and steam ships by 1901. In almost every sphere of activity, be it education, travel, industry, agriculture or commerce, the changes were wide-ranging.

One of the most startling changes was in the growth of towns; for some of the prosperous towns and cities of the early twentieth century had been obscure hamlets when Victoria came to the throne. Towns like Middlesbrough, Barrow-in-Furness and Crewe were the products of Victorian industry.

It was also a time of continuous colonial expeditions and these are reflected in house and street names such as Gordon Villas, Khartoum, Ashanti Street and Kabul Road. There were innumerable wars, including three in Ashanti (Ghana) and two in Afghanistan; but relatively few memorials to the soldiers and sailors who died in uniform. The Indian Mutiny of 1857 was celebrated in a number of ways, not least for the cruelty with which the army put down the mutiny afterwards. Many soldiers received the Victoria Cross yet there are relatively few war memorials to the 11 000 British soldiers who died during the campaign.

The Crimean War

The Crimean War was the first major war since the battle of Waterloo. Lord Raglan, leader of the British Expeditionary Force, had lost his arm at Waterloo as a young officer serving at the side of the Duke of Wellington. The army, stores and equipment he took to the Crimea in 1854 proved grossly inadequate. Public outcry during the war

helped to bring some changes afterwards to the army; not least in the provision of adequate nursing for the wounded. It was the heroism of the soldiers in the fighting which prompted the founding of the Victoria Cross.

Like the Indian Mutiny, memorials to the men who died are few and far between. The best example is the memorial to the Brigade of Guards in Waterloo Place in London and the adjacent memorial to Florence Nightingale with its scenes depicting her life's work.

The Crimean War was fought at a time when many new streets were being built in Britain's towns. It is not surprising therefore to find that in some districts a series of streets all have names with Crimean associations such as Raglan Street, Cardigan Street (he led the Charge of the Light Brigade) and Alma Street (this was the first battle of the Crimean War). Alma became a girl's forename from this time onward. The gravestone of a baby girl with the Christian names Frances Alma, who was born about six months after the battle of the Alma, can be seen in Grasmere churchyard in Cumbria.

Bronze relief depicting a Ninth Lancer (9L on saddle) on the monument in Exeter Cathedral to the men who died during the Indian Mutiny in 1857.

The Railways

In 1825 George Stephenson successfully carried passengers from Shildon (near Darlington) to Stockton in a railway train pulled by his engine *Locomotion*. The original of this locomotive can be seen in the North Road Station Museum in Darlington and a working model can be seen on the railway line at the North of England Open Air Museum at Beamish in County Durham.

In 1830 Stephenson's trains started the world's first scheduled passenger railway service between Liverpool and Manchester. Within 20 years Britain was criss-crossed with a network of 6000 miles of railway lines.

Among the great pioneers of the railway was the engineer Isambard Kingdom Brunel whose achievements also included steamships (the largest ship in the world – *The Great Eastern*), bridges (Clifton Suspension) and the Great Western Railway. One of his more enduring monuments is the Royal Albert Railway Bridge across the Tamar between Saltash and Plymouth. The railway deck is suspended from the two great tubular arches made of iron.

Early railway travel was much more of a hardship then than it is today. There were no buffet cars and trains made scheduled stops of ten min-

Crimean War memorial to the Brigade of Guards in Waterloo Place, London.

Memorial to Florence Nightingale in Waterloo Place.

utes or so to allow passengers to invade the refreshment rooms. There were no electric lights then and the dim light thrown by oil lamps was inadequate. Passengers had to be on their guard against thieves. There was no heating either and no lavatories.

Even so, despite the contrasts between the standard of railway travel in the 1850s and that of the present day, the railway stations themselves don't seem to have changed much in the course of 150 years. A Victorian passenger arriving at Newcastle's Central Station today wouldn't notice much amiss. Engravings of Victorian railway stations, even as early as those of 1840, show familiar sights such as the station clock and the left luggage room.

Working model of George Stephenson's Locomotion at the North of England Open Air Museum at Beamish, County Durham.

Travel

The Victorian era owed a great deal to the horse. Despite the use of steam on the railways the horse was still the prime mover over land for the rest of the nineteenth century, although surprisingly few of the horse troughs, which provided the Victorian equivalent of a filling station, remain. Mews cottages converted from former stables are, however, one reminder in London of the importance of horse-drawn transport in the nineteenth century.

Horse buses were introduced in 1829 and soon caught the imagination of the public. No photograph of Victorian London seems complete without one; which makes it all the more odd that so little evidence, of their massive presence on the streets of Victorian Britain, can be seen today. In 1861 the first horse-drawn trams were seen in London, as they can still be seen today on the Isle of Man.

Horse-drawn cabs provided an alternative form of transport in towns. The 'growler' was a conventional four-wheeled cab with the driver sitting in front but the 'hansom' gave a more exciting ride since it was faster, more manoeuvrable and the view was unobstructed (the driver sat on a perch at the back of the cab). The hansom was introduced to London at about the same time as the horse bus. The Hansom Cab public house in Earl's Court Road in London features an inn sign, a cab hood and also a carriage light.

Cheap public transport fostered the growth of

Royal Albert Railway Bridge at Saltash, Cornwall.

BELOW *Entrance to Huddersfield's classical railway station built in 1847.*

large cities since it enabled people to live at a distance away from their place of work. The first London Underground services began in 1863 with the opening of the Metropolitan Line but it was not until 1890 that the Tube made its greatest impact when the first electric underground railway came into service.

It was at about this time that the electric tram first began to be seen on the roads and streets of Britain. Travel by electric tram was cheaper than by horse bus and with the Underground it provided the first really cheap form of public transport.

The period between 1880 and 1905 was very much a quarter of a century of change – a transport revolution which saw the introduction and development of the motor car, motor bus, electric underground railway, electric tram, safety bicycle and aeroplane.

Few reminders of these golden days of transport innovation can be seen today outside the museums, although Blackpool still has its electric trams and a number of the ancient black and yellow AA road signs can also be seen.

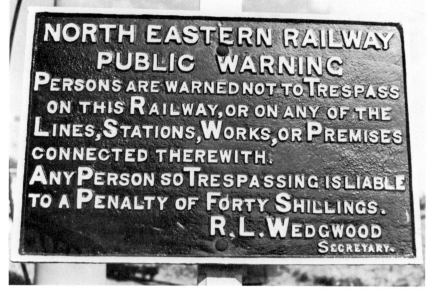

Warning sign on the railway at the North of England Open Air Museum at Beamish.

BELOW *Newcastle-upon-Tyne's Central Station, built in about 1850.*

ABOVE LEFT *Horse trough at Ledbury, Herefordshire.*

ABOVE AND LEFT *The Hansom Cab public house in Earl's Court Road, London.*

BELOW *Automobile Association plaque on the wall of a house in Kersey in Suffolk.*

SHOP at BINNS
FOR EVERYTHING

Tram at the North of England Open Air Museum at Beamish, County Durham.

Victorian Streets

Many of the early nineteenth-century houses, built for miners and factory workers, were erected around a central courtyard with the minimal amenities of a communal tap and a privy. Fortunately these courts have long since been pulled down. Indeed some were cleared when the railways were built between 100 and 150 years ago. Charles Dickens described the process in *Dombey and Son* in 1847: 'Houses were knocked down; streets broken through and stopped; deep pits and trenches dug in the ground; enormous heaps of earth and clay thrown up.'

Despite their look-alike appearance there is usually more in the Victorian street than meets the eye and the ways in which the houses have been individualized by successive occupiers can be fascinating to detect. It would be a pity if urban redevelopment eventually led to the loss of the Victorian suburbs, for they are as much a part of our living heritage as the half-timbered houses of Lavenham or the Georgian terraces of Bath.

Since this was a period of rapid growth the building of new streets of houses meant that many new street names were needed each year. As a result a walk through the Victorian part of town can become a history lesson. It doesn't require a high degree of skill to date a group of streets in Kentish Town in London with the names Raglan Street, Alma Street and Inkerman Road. Rather more research might be needed, however, in south Ealing to put a date on Blondin Avenue and Niagara Avenue.

Pub signs such as the *Jack the Ripper* in Spitalfields (where he murdered his last victim) and the few surviving gas street lights evoke the atmosphere of Victorian London. Plaques and other

Victorian terraced street at Farnley in Leeds.

BELOW *Street of terraced houses in Newcastle-upon-Tyne.*

additions to house walls are not without interest either. On a house in Goudhurst in Kent there are three stone carvings made by a Victorian stone mason, perhaps as a specimen of his work and at various points in London it is possible to see the parish boundary marks. Typical is the one to be seen on the wall of St James's Palace.

Gas lamp in a courtyard off St James's Street, London.

Victorian Street Furniture

The various additions to a street, such as postboxes and bollards, are collectively known as 'street furniture'. These often provide interesting sidelights on the nature of everyday life in the past.

Footscrapers vividly bring home the reality of the Georgian or Victorian street with its horse-drawn traffic. Roads and pavements were often filthy, particularly in bad weather; so enterprising children (and adults) set themselves up as crossing sweepers, earning a few pennies by sweeping clear paths across the streets for the more-affluent pedestrians. The footscraper today is something of an unnecessary luxury outside a town home, but it still justifies its place at the farm door.

TOP *Stone carving on a house in Goudhurst in Kent.*

ABOVE *Boundary marks on the wall of St James's Palace, London.*

TOP *Footscraper in Saffron Walden in Essex.*

ABOVE *Tethering ring on a mounting block in Alston, Cumbria.*

RIGHT *Iron bollard protecting the corner of a building in St Andrews, Fifeshire. Stones placed in this position are called spur stones.*

ABOVE LEFT *Bollards protecting the sides of a building in Alston, Cumbria.*

ABOVE *Porters' rest in Piccadilly, London. Servants, workmen and porters carrying heavy loads could rest them temporarily here.*

LEFT *Victorian drinking fountain with a cast iron shelter at Nenthead in Cumbria. It was donated by the London Lead Company, the major employer in the area.*

ABOVE *Ornamental street light in Waterloo Place, London.*

LEFT *Unusual milestone at Horsebridge in Sussex. The four cast iron bells represent Bow Bells; so it is 53 miles to London!*

Early Victorian letter box with vertical slit – in Framlingham, Suffolk.

Memorial to Grace Darling in the churchyard at Bamburgh in Northumberland.

Churches and Chapels

Victorian churches can be seen mainly in the towns, since it was there rather than in the countryside, that the huge increase in population in the nineteenth century took place. Most industrial towns have a number of churches founded in the Victorian period, many of them of little real distinction.

However, the Victorians had something specific to contribute to ecclesiastical architecture with the spread of Methodism and the other Nonconformist denominations. A surprisingly high number of the nonconformist chapels and churches were built with a triangular pediment across the front of the building together with tall round-arched windows.

Many people find Victorian churchyards of greater interest than the buildings. In Postmen's Park, the churchyard of St Botolph Aldersgate near the post office in St Martin's-le-Grand, there are over 50 tablets commemorating the heroism of

Hooped graves at Warden in Northumberland.

BELOW *Baptist church built in the 1860s in Ross-on-Wye in Herefordshire.*

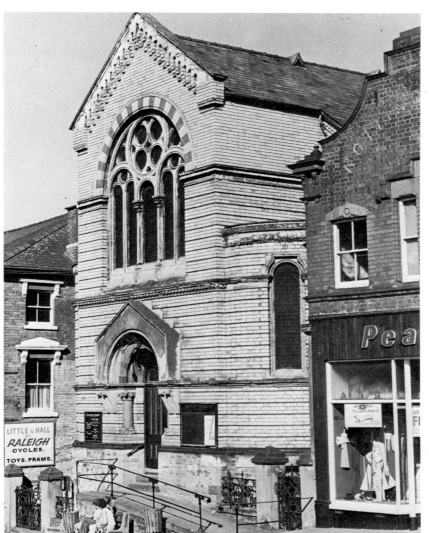

ordinary people in Victorian times. Elaborate Gothic memorials like that of Grace Darling in the churchyard at Bamburgh in Northumberland epitomize the Victorian attitude to death, closely resembling, as it does, the Victorian hearse and only lacking its black caparisoned horses.

The hooped graves at Warden in Northumberland have another Victorian tale to tell since the hoops were designed to stop body-snatchers from selling the corpses to a medical school for dissection.

Schools

Many children are still taught in buildings which are a form of living history in themselves! Victorian schools, like the one in Snettisham in Norfolk, are often double-gabled with large imitation Gothic windows and a central bell tower. Little imagination is needed to picture the Wakefield school as it might have looked in 1890 when it was built.

The 1870 Education Act resulted in the formation of local school boards which had the power to levy a rate and to erect new schools if these were needed. Many villages and towns already had schools which had been founded on a voluntary basis by organizations such as the British School Society which was Nonconformist and the National Society which was Anglican. A number of the buildings used by these schools can still be seen in different parts of Britain but most of the existing schools built in the nineteenth century date from after 1870. In the large towns they often had several storeys with large classrooms holding upwards of 60 to 70 pupils.

ABOVE *Victorian school (1890) in Wakefield, west Yorkshire.*   BELOW *Village school (1875) at Snettisham, Norfolk.*

Public Buildings

It has often been remarked that the exuberant confidence of the Victorians (or at least that of those Victorians who had made or inherited wealth) was best displayed in their public buildings. These huge and impressive structures were built to inspire confidence. There were no half measures. Designs submitted by architects for the construction of government buildings in London were never less than grand, while at the same time showing an obsession with decorative detail.

Many Victorian public buildings, like the Town Hall in Bolton (1873) and the Corn Exchange in Bury St Edmunds (1862), are classical in conception. The Royal Albert Hall, which was opened in 1871, has a terracotta frieze encircling the dome depicting the history of the arts and sciences.

The Houses of Parliament, however, are Gothic in design. The old Palace of Westminster was destroyed by fire on 16 October 1834 and when a competition for a new design was announced it was stipulated that the design had to be either Gothic in style or Elizabethan – not Roman or Greek. Gothic won. The building was mainly constructed between 1840 and 1850, opened by Queen Victoria in 1852 and not finally completed until 1857.

Bolton Town Hall, built in 1873.

BELOW *The County Sessions House in Liverpool, completed in 1884.*

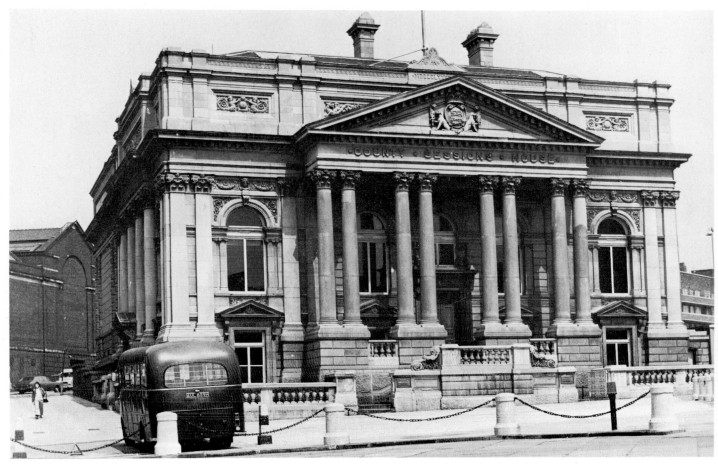

The Royal Albert Hall, opened in 1871.

BELOW *The Corn Exchange, Bury St Edmunds (1862).*

Recreations and Holidays

One of the most remarkable developments of the Victorian period was the speed with which the opportunities and amenities for recreation and pleasure multiplied – at odds perhaps with the conventional view of the Victorians as sober, industrious and puritanical.

The nineteenth century saw the rapid development of the music hall from modest places of refreshment, enlivened by songs, to the many new variety theatres of the 1890s. It was a time when municipal parks were constructed on a lavish scale with ornamental fountains, summer houses and ornate circular bandstands.

The Victorian period also saw the remarkable emergence of professional sport. Many of the major world sports of today were either invented or developed out of all recognition in Victorian Britain. Football, which was a rough uninhibited game in the 1830s, was duly codified into Association, Rugby Union and Rugby League football in the 1860s, 1870s and 1890s respectively. Cricket was transformed. In the 1830s batsmen were still scoring notches and the game had hardly developed beyond the village green. Seventy years later the game drew large crowds to the England and Australia test matches. Golf was another game which developed from a local sport in Scotland to one with an international following by 1900. The first British Open Championship was held at Prestwick in 1860.

Lawn tennis in something approaching its modern form was first played by T. H. Gem and J. B. Perera in Birmingham in the 1860s whilst table tennis began 'with champagne corks, cut as nearly circular as possible, using the lids of cigar boxes as battledores'.

Edwardian bandstand in the North of England Open Air Museum at Beamish, County Durham.

Victorian public house in Oldham, Lancashire.

the ordinary working person, despite Queen Victoria's love affair with the area.

The most striking change came with the development of the railways. Cheap day excursion tickets to the coast enabled thousands of Lancashire trippers to board huge excursion trains bound for Blackpool or the Lake District. The invasion of day trippers by train to Windermere and then by steamer to Ambleside worried Lake District residents so much, that they successfully opposed an 1880 proposal to extend the railway

RIGHT *Memorial to Tom Morris, Junior – four times Open Golf Champion – in the churchyard at St Andrews, Fifeshire.*

The Victorians also invented the Bank Holiday which was first celebrated in 1871. Holy days in the Middle Ages had been frequent and the occasion for local entertainment. But isolated holidays like this were an impediment to the smooth working of a factory, to say nothing of its profits. Structured holidays became the order of the day.

At the same time the development of cheap travel paved the way for the day trip and ultimately the seaside holiday. In the golden age of coaching only the well-to-do could afford to travel to the newly developed health resorts of Brighton, Scarborough and Weymouth. Nor were the attractions of Scotland and its Highlands for

to Ambleside. Many seaside resorts were created by the railway companies such as Cleethorpes and Skegness, while others like Blackpool and Bournemouth only flourished when linked by railway line to the major centres of population.

Piers, theatres, hotels and promenades proliferated, so much so that most seafronts, even today, are essentially late Victorian or Edwardian in character.

ABOVE *Palace Pier, Brighton, built at the turn of the century in about 1899.*

RIGHT *Stone commemorating the visit of Queen Victoria in 1877 to Loch Maree. The Queen remained six nights at the Loch Maree Hotel 'and in her Gracious Condescension willed that this stone should be a remembrancer of the pleasure she found in coming to this part of Ross-shire'.*

Gravestone, of one of the pioneers of the seaside holiday, in a Brighton churchyard. The bather 'helped' to persuade reluctant swimmers to enter the water!

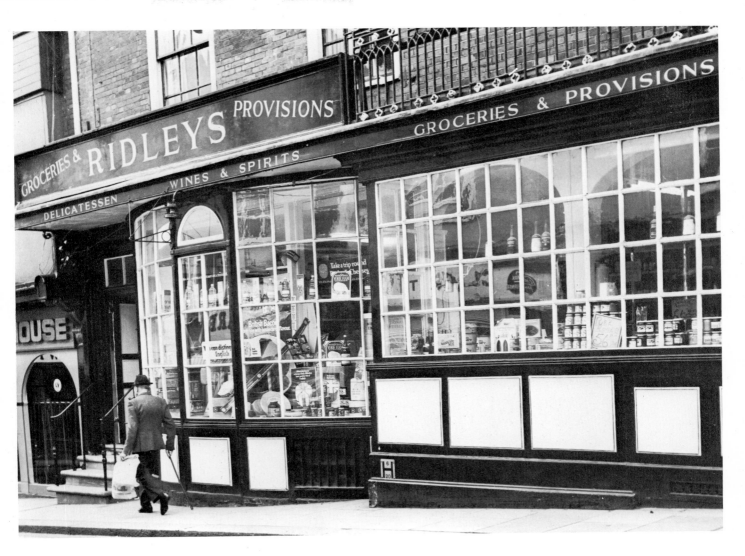

Shops and Shopping

By 1900 the development of cheap transport enabled people living in the outer suburbs to travel to the town centre to shop. Fifty years earlier most people would have had to make such a journey on foot.

Entrepreneurs seized the opportunity presented by this change in shopping habits and built departmental stores in the large cities. Chain stores were started from humble beginnings. Jesse Boot opened a small chemist's shop in Nottingham and W. H. Smith, anticipating that the travelling public would need something to read on the trains, opened a chain of shops selling books and newspapers on railway stations.

Unhappily the façades and trimmings of the typical Victorian shop are fast disappearing although it is still possible to put the clock back in a shopping arcade or covered market such as Newcastle's Central Arcade built in 1906 or London's Leadenhall Market built in 1881. Ridleys grocery in Bury St Edmunds looks much the same today as it did when photographed in the 1890s.

The Edwardian Era

The first 14 years of the twentieth century began with the disastrous South African War, the last to be widely commemorated in street names (such as Mafeking Avenue and Ladysmith Terrace). War memorials to the soldiers who died then are more widespread than those of the Crimean War but still fairly thin on the ground.

The period leading up to the start of the Great War was a time of rapid social change. Despite the prominence given to the activities of the suffragettes there are relatively few reminders today to recall the work of the movement. Even the gravestone of Emily Wilding Davison, who threw herself under the King's horse at the 1913 Derby, carries no indication that she was a member of the suffragette movement. Instead, by an ironic and poignant twist, this monument to a prominent feminist begins 'Greater love hath no man than this, that a man lay down his life for his friends'.

LEFT *Central Arcade, Newcastle-upon-Tyne.*

ABOVE *Victorian shop in Bury St Edmunds, Suffolk.*

APPLEBY
ACTIVE SERVICE VOLUNTEERS.
IN SOUTH AFRICA 1900.1.
THOMAS LEONARD ATKINSON
THOMAS HENRY DAVEY
THOMAS GIBSON
THOMAS HOLMES
RICHARD HOWE
THOMAS HOWE
HARRY ROBINSON
JOSEPH SAUL
EDWARD WALTON SLACK
WILLIAM THOMAS TYDO
WILLIAM JAMES WOOF.

GREATER LOVE HATH NO MAN
THAN THIS, THAT A MAN LAY
DOWN HIS LIFE FOR HIS
FRIENDS. ST JOHN XV CHR XIII VERSE.

EMILY WILDING
DAVISON,
BORN OCT 11th 1872,
DIED JUNE 8th 1913.

"DEEDS, NOT WORDS."

ALFRED NORRIS
DAVISON,

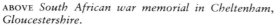

ABOVE *South African war memorial in Cheltenham, Gloucestershire.*

ABOVE RIGHT *South African war memorial in Appleby, Cumbria.*

RIGHT *Emily Wilding Davison's tombstone in a Morpeth churchyard, Northumberland.*

The Great War

The Great War, which brought four years of suffering and the deaths of nearly one million soldiers, was so universally commemorated that it is easy to gloss over the reality behind the plaques in schools and factories or the obelisks and memorial gardens. For many towns a simple cenotaph was sufficient, for others a more elaborate memorial portrayed soldiers, civilians and sometimes even weapons.

Simpler but no less poignant memorials to the war include the simple wooden crosses which hang on a wall in Salisbury Cathedral and the grave of Edith Cavell in a quiet corner outside Norwich Cathedral.

An unusual and unexpected Great War monument can be seen in the churchyard of the Suffolk village of Theberton, where a fragment from a German Zeppelin can be seen inside the church porch. In the churchyard on the other side of the road a memorial marks the spot where the 16 members of the Zeppelin's crew were buried in 1917.

TOP *War memorial in Newcastle-upon-Tyne, showing working men departing for the war in 1914.*

ABOVE RIGHT *Simple wooden crosses hanging on the walls of Salisbury Cathedral – for a soldier who died in Palestine (left) and at the battle of the Somme (right).*

RIGHT *Tombstone to Edith Cavell who was executed by the Germans in Belgium in 1915. Norwich Cathedral.*

Royal Artillery war memorial at Hyde Park Corner featuring a huge gun at the summit of the monument – dramatic but hardly appropriate.

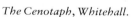
The Cenotaph, Whitehall.

HERE WERE BURIED 16 GERMAN AIRMEN CREW OF ZEPPELIN L 48 17TH JUNE 1917 "WHO ART THOU THAT JUDGEST ANOTHER MANS SERVANT." ROM. XIV-IV.

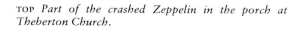
TOP *Part of the crashed Zeppelin in the porch at Theberton Church.*

ABOVE *Memorial plaque in the churchyard at Theberton in Suffolk.*

The Twentieth Century

Statue of David Lloyd George outside Caernarfon Castle.

Statue of Winston Churchill in Parliament Square, Westminster.

In any future history of twentieth-century Britain the life and work of Winston Churchill and David Lloyd George will be sure to find an important place.

Whether the twentieth century will leave much else for later generations to venerate as part of their continuing heritage is a matter of some interest. In a hundred years' time the remains of multi-storeyed car parks, filling stations and motorways may well be regarded with much the same interest then as we view a tollhouse or turnpike road today.

Many of the buildings of the twentieth century will no doubt survive, perhaps deliberately chosen by an increasingly conservation-conscious society, dictating to posterity how their generation should be viewed.

Index

Note: Page numbers in *italics* indicate a photograph.

Brief Acknowledgement

I owe an enormous debt of gratitude to sources of information far too innumerable to mention individually by name. They range from guidebooks, gazetteers, social histories, topographical guides and visitors' guides to castles, abbeys, churches and historic houses on the one hand, to the helpful and illuminating advice and encouragement of wardens, curators and ticket collectors on the other – to say nothing of the support I have received on location from the long-suffering, if not always silent, members of my family!